First World War
and Army of Occupation
War Diary
France, Belgium and Germany

41 DIVISION
Divisional Troops
187 Brigade Royal Field Artillery
1 May 1916 - 25 October 1919

WO95/2625/2

The Naval & Military Press Ltd
www.nmarchive.com
Published in association with The National Archives

Published by

The Naval & Military Press Ltd

Unit 10 Ridgewood Industrial Park,

Uckfield, East Sussex,

TN22 5QE England

Tel: +44 (0) 1825 749494

www.naval-military-press.com

www.nmarchive.com

This diary has been reprinted in facsimile from the original. Any imperfections are inevitably reproduced and the quality may fall short of modern type and cartographic standards.

© Crown Copyright
Images reproduced by permission of The National Archives, London, England, 2015.

Contents

Document type	Place/Title	Date From	Date To
Heading	41st Division 187th Brigade R.F.A. May 1916-Oct 1917 Mar 1918-1919 Oct In Italy 1917 Nov-1918 Feb		
Heading	WO95/2625/2 41 Div 187 Bde RFA May 1916-Oct 1917		
War Diary	Ewshot	01/05/1916	01/05/1916
War Diary	Havre	02/05/1916	03/05/1916
War Diary	Hazebrouck	03/05/1916	03/05/1916
War Diary	Caestre.	05/05/1916	27/05/1916
War Diary	Nieppe.	05/06/1916	12/06/1916
War Diary	Nieppe	09/06/1916	30/06/1916
War Diary	B.11.d.5.8.	02/07/1916	28/07/1916
War Diary	Nieppe	01/08/1916	24/08/1916
War Diary	Pont Remy	27/08/1916	01/09/1916
War Diary	Ailly Sur Somme	02/09/1916	02/09/1916
War Diary	Dernancourt	03/09/1916	12/09/1916
War Diary	Positions as given above.	13/09/1916	15/09/1916
War Diary	S.11.b.	16/09/1916	30/09/1916
War Diary	S.16.c.22.	01/10/1916	15/10/1916
War Diary		14/10/1916	16/10/1916
War Diary		15/10/1916	28/10/1916
War Diary	Dernancourt	01/11/1916	30/11/1916
War Diary	Dickebusch	01/12/1916	31/12/1916
War Diary	St. Eloi	01/04/1917	30/04/1917
Miscellaneous	War Diary Of 187th. Brigade R.F.A. For March 1917.	27/04/1917	27/04/1917
War Diary	Dickebusch	01/05/1917	05/05/1917
War Diary	La Clytte	05/05/1917	27/05/1917
War Diary	La Clytte	07/05/1917	28/05/1917
War Diary	Dickebusch	28/05/1917	31/05/1917
Heading	41st Division Diary of 187 Bde R.F.A. for June '17 is missing		
Miscellaneous			
War Diary	Dead Dog Farm.	01/07/1917	06/07/1917
War Diary	Boeschepe.	07/07/1917	19/07/1917
War Diary	St. Eloi.	20/07/1917	31/07/1917
Map	Batty Positions For Offensive Appendix I		
Map	Group Zones for Offensives Appendix II		
Miscellaneous	Night Firing 20/21st July Reference:- Hollebeke 1/10.000 German trenches corrected to 29/6/17 Appendix III	20/07/1917	20/07/1917
Miscellaneous	To Officer Commanding, Bluff Group.	20/07/1917	20/07/1917
Miscellaneous	41st Divisional Artillery Instructions No. 6 Appendix IV	17/07/1917	17/07/1917
Miscellaneous	Night Firing July 21/22nd. Appendix V	21/07/1917	21/07/1917
Miscellaneous	Extract from 47th. Intelligence Summary.	21/07/1917	21/07/1917
Map	Principal Roads Used		
Operation(al) Order(s)	St. Eloi Artillery Group Operation Order No. 1 Appendix VI	22/07/1917	22/07/1917
Operation(al) Order(s)	St Eloi Artillery Group Operation Order No. 2. Appendix VII	23/07/1917	23/07/1917
Miscellaneous	Amendment To Operation Order No. 2.	23/07/1917	23/07/1917
Operation(al) Order(s)	St Eloi Artillery Operation Order No. 3 Appendix VIII	25/07/1917	25/07/1917

Miscellaneous	Battle Wood Group Appendix IX	26/07/1917	26/07/1917
Miscellaneous	41st Divl. Arty. Special Instruction No. 6. Appendix X	27/07/1917	27/07/1917
Miscellaneous	41st D.A., Special Instructions For 29th July 1917 Appendix XI	29/07/1917	29/07/1917
Miscellaneous	From:- Adjutant St. Eloi Artillery Group. To:- Officers Commanding Batteries. Appendix XII	30/07/1917	30/07/1917
Miscellaneous	From:- Adjutant St Eloi Artillery Group. To:- Officers Commanding Batteries. Appendix XIII	30/07/1917	30/07/1917
Miscellaneous	Amendment To Standing Barrage Table.	30/07/1917	30/07/1917
Miscellaneous	Creeping Barrage. Table.	23/07/1917	23/07/1917
Miscellaneous	Amendment To Creeping Barrage Table.	30/07/1917	30/07/1917
Miscellaneous	Amendment To Standing And Creeping Barrage.	28/07/1917	28/07/1917
Miscellaneous	4.5" Howitzer Standing Barrage.	23/07/1917	23/07/1917
Miscellaneous	18-Pdr. Standing Barrage.	23/07/1917	23/07/1917
Miscellaneous	Addendum To Barrage Tables.	24/07/1917	24/07/1917
Miscellaneous	41st. Divisional Artillery Instruction No. 8. App. XIV	20/07/1917	20/07/1917
Miscellaneous	Memorandum	25/07/1917	25/07/1917
Map	Map "G"		
War Diary		01/08/1917	31/10/1917
Heading	WO95/2625/3 41 Div 187 Bde RFA March 1918-Oct 1919		
Heading	41st Div. Bde. returned with Div. from Italy 8/13.3.18. Headquarters, 187th Brigade, R.F.A. March 1918		
War Diary	Italy	01/03/1918	09/03/1918
War Diary	France	12/03/1918	31/03/1918
Heading	41st Divisional Artillery 187th Brigade R.F.A. April 1918		
War Diary	France	01/04/1918	30/11/1918
War Diary	Belgium	01/12/1918	31/01/1919
War Diary	Germany.	01/02/1919	25/04/1919
War Diary	Germany.	10/04/1919	31/05/1919
War Diary	Germany.	01/05/1919	30/06/1919
War Diary	Germany.	01/06/1919	19/07/1919
War Diary	Germany	01/07/1919	01/09/1919
War Diary	Kalk Near Cologne Germany	14/10/1919	25/10/1919
Miscellaneous	Movements Of Officers-October 1919. 187th Brigade, Royal Field Artillery.	25/10/1919	25/10/1919
War Diary	Kalk Near Cologne Germany	14/10/1919	25/10/1919
Miscellaneous	Movements Of Officers-October 1919. 187th Brigade, Royal Field Artillery.	25/10/1919	25/10/1919

41ST DIVISION

187TH BRIGADE R.F.A.

MAY 1916 - ~~DEC 1918.~~ OCT 1917
MAR 1918 — 1919 OCT

IN ITALY
1917 NOV — 1918 FEB

WO 95/2625/2
41 DIV
187 BDE RFA
Army 1916 - Oct 1917

Vol 1

Army Form C. 2118

WAR DIARY or INTELLIGENCE SUMMARY

(Erase heading not required.)

187th. Brigade, R.F.A.

Place	Date	Hour	Summary of Events and Information	Remarks and references to Appendices
Bristol	1/5/16	2.15am to 9.00am	187th Brigade R.F.A, proceeded to entrain at Avonmouth for Southampton. From thence embarked for Havre.	A.W.D.
Havre	2/5/16	8.30 am.	Arrived Havre, where the Brigade stayed the night at Rest Camp No. 5.	A.W.D.
Havre	3/5/16	8.0am.	Entrained for Hazebrouck, and detrained at 8.0 am 4/5/16.	A.W.D.
Hazebrouck	4/5/16	8.0am.	Detrained and took up billets as follows:—	A.W.D.
			Headquarters — — — W. 3. a. 1. 8. Caestre.	
			"A" Battery — — — P. 36. c. 2. 5.	
			" do — — — W. 9. Central.	Reference map
			"B" do — — — W. 9. 6. 4. 4.	Sheet 27. 1/10.000
			"C" do — — — W. 9. 6. 2. 9.	
			"D" do — — — W. 2. c. 3. 0	
			B.A.C.	
Caestre	5/5/16		Units in same billets.	A.W.D.
"	6/5/16		do	A.W.D.
"	7/5/16		do do Commanding Officer made reconnaissance of positions now occupied by 50th Brigade R.F.A, which will be taken over by this Brigade.	A.W.D.
"	8/5/16		A gun detachment each from "A", "B", "C" & "D" Batteries of this Brigade took over the positions occupied respectively by a gun detachment of "A", "B", "C", "D" Batteries 50th Brigade R.F.A. for registration and instructional purposes.	A.W.D. A.W.D.
"	27/5/16		Remainder of 187th. Brigade proceeded into positions, and took over from 50th Brigade R.F.A. B.A.C. billets a/a, and groups of Batteries formed. Lieut: Colonel R.S.M. Head, Commanding 187th Brigade R.F.A, now has under his command the following Batteries:—	A.W.D.

WAR DIARY or INTELLIGENCE SUMMARY

Army Form C. 2118

(Erase heading not required.)

Place	Date	Hour	Summary of Events and Information	Remarks and references to Appendices
Nieppe	5/6/16		Fired 500 rounds all calibre guns on TL "BIRDCAGE" U.22.C.4.3, a strong enemy position, with good effect.	A/H.O
	8/6/16		Took on all gun positions, strengthening etc., is being carried on with all speed.	C/H.O
	12/6/16		D/187 fired 60 rounds on FORT U.26.b.6.7 with good effect, causing considerable damage.	A/H.O
	13/6/16	12 mnt.	A/187 fired 60 rounds on FORT U.28.a.4.6 in conjunction with infantry operations, with good effect. Enemy did not retaliate, but gunfire a considerable distance north eastward increased, and probably developed into an engagement. Enemy sent up many Very lights.	A/H.O
	14/6/16	11.0pm	All clocks advanced 60 minutes, and 11.0pm became 12.0 midnight 14/15th June 1916.	A/H.O
	16/6/16	11.50pm	Very heavy bombardment heard to the aft of our sector.	B/H.O
	17/6/16	12.20am	Gas alarms heard, and taken up by this group. Necessary precautionary measures taken. Gas slightly felt.	D/H.O
		12.50am	No S.O.S. received, but on receipt of gas alarm batteries opened fire.	C/H.O
		1.30am	Normal conditions resumed, and remainder of day quiet.	S/H.O
	18/6/16		Fairly quiet day.	C/H.O
		11.55pm	Shouts were heard sounding gas alarm; necessary precautions taken. Batteries reported no gas on their front, and all quiet.	A/H.O
	19/6/16	12.15am	B/187 received S.O.S. from infantry and opened fire.	A/H.O
		12.25am	A/187 fired S.O.S. Normal conditions resumed.	A/H.O
		12.40am		
		7.30pm	Quiet day up to this time.	C/H.O
	20/6/16	6.32-6.34 pm	Bombardment by A/187, B/187 & C/187 preliminary to infantry making smoke attack. Effect unsuccessful, and had desired effect. 240 rounds fired 30% each A & K.	C/H.O
	21/6/16	6.2-6.4 pm	Bombarded by A/187, B/187 & C/187. Fired 9 rounds per gun, 30% each A & K. Effective, but owing to smaller number of rounds being fired, not so much damage was done. This was in conjunction with smoke attack by infantry.	A/H.O
	22/6/16	11.32pm	Gas alarm heard, and necessary precautions taken. All batteries opened fire on seeing red rocket, which was also reported as being some from German lines. No battery received S.O.S. rocket call.	A/H.O

Army Form C. 2118

WAR DIARY
or
INTELLIGENCE SUMMARY

(Erase heading not required.)

Instructions regarding War Diaries and Intelligence Summaries are contained in F. S. Regs., Part II. and the Staff Manual respectively. Title Pages will be prepared in manuscript.

Place	Date	Hour	Summary of Events and Information	Remarks and references to Appendices
MEPPE	30/6/16	7.00 pm	Batteries commenced wire cutting in front of enemy trenches, which was successfully carried out.	AKW
		9.15 pm	Bombardment on enemy trenches and support trenches commenced. Ceased fire for 15 minutes.	AKW
		9.45 pm		
		10.0 pm	Bombarded until 10.28 pm. At 10.28 lifted and barraged.	AKW
			The above operation was carried out in connection with infantry etc. after discharge of gas, made a raid on enemy trenches. The whole operation extended from ... to ... on the front covered by the 4th [?] Divis was successfully carried out.	AMO

41

Army Form C. 2118

WAR DIARY
or
~~INTELLIGENCE SUMMARY~~

(Erase heading not required.)

Centre Group R.F.A. / (187th Brigade R.F.A. & B/183.)   July 1916   Vol 3

Place	Date	Hour	Summary of Events and Information	Remarks and references to Appendices
B.11.d.5.8.	night July 2/3		Following shoot ordered by C.R.A. 41st Division to be carried out. Fire on roads used by enemy, special attention being paid to Cross Roads. Centre Group area South of line U.16—17—18 Central. Ammunition to be used 2000 rounds 18 pdr shrapnel, and for counter battery work 200 rounds 4.5" How. H.E.	Maps
do.	9/7/16		Instructed by C.R.A. 41st Division that, on each night when Divisional Artillery is not cooperating in raids, short sharp bursts of fire will be made from different batteries at different times on hostile support line. Up to 100 rounds 18 pdr (50% shrapnel & 50% H.E.) may be used per group each night. Batteries chosen for this work are A/187, B/183, B/187 and C/187.	Maps
do	night 10/11		Divisional Artillery cooperated with Infantry, who were to make a point in hostile trenches opposite T.123, the object being to capture prisoners and do as much damage as possible.	Maps
do.	night 12/13. 14/7/16		Wire cutting operations B/183 objective U.15.a.7.6. 6/4 to U.15.a. 9.4.6. Rounds to be fired 400 shrapnel	Maps
do.	15/7/16		Re night shoots ordered on 9/7/16 — now cancelled. Tests carried out by D/187 with powder filled shells. They were found to give no flash but a lot of smoke. Very useful at night time as guns cannot be located by flash, but useless for day work.	Maps
do.	19/7/16		Ammunition held by Batteries to be reduced to:— 18 Pdr. 4.5" How. With gun. 200. 100. Wagon lines. 176. 108.	Maps
do	21/7/16		Daily expenditure of ammunition to be used down to per 18 pdr battery 9 rounds per gun per day, 4.5" How. NIL., except in cases of real emergency.	Maps

Army Form C. 2118

WAR DIARY
or
INTELLIGENCE SUMMARY

(Erase heading not required.)

R.F.A. Centre Group R.F.A.
(187th Brigade R.F.A.)
July 1916.

Place	Date	Hour	Summary of Events and Information	Remarks and references to Appendices
B.11.d.5.8	22/7/16		Batteries ordered to report on battery positions, by C.R.A. W/St Division, as follows; in view of future operations:—	ANO
			Number. Position. Centre line. Tested by.	
			H. 29. U.21.a.7.8. DECOMINCK FARM. B/183.	ANO
			H. 30. U.15.c.3.3. do. A/187.	
			H. 31. U.15.c.½.5. do. C/187.	
			H. 32. U.14.c.9.1. do. B/187.	
			L. 9. C.1.b.8½.2. U.17.c.9.0. D/187	
			L. 10. C.2.c.0.4. U.23.a.6½.3. do	
			L. 11. C.2.d.2.0. do. do.	
do.	23/7/16		Regarding 134th. Infantry Brigade Minor Enterprise 26th. instant, Batteries ordered to cut wire as follows:—	ANO
			B/183. U.22.a.3½.5 to U.22.c.3.3.	
			B/167. U.22.c.3.3. to U.22.c.4½.2.	
			A/187. U.22.c.4½.2 to U.22.c.5.1.	
do.	Night 23/24		"WYKEHAM" Screens, and dummy gun positions erected at following positions:—	ANO
			U.26.b.9.1.	
			U.26.d.5.2.	
			C.2.c.3.3.	
			U.26.c.5.7.	
			Reports to be made if these draw enemy fire.	

Army Form C. 2118

WAR DIARY or INTELLIGENCE SUMMARY

(Erase heading not required.)

Centre Group R.F.A. (18th Brigade R.F.A.) July 1916.

Place	Date	Hour	Summary of Events and Information	Remarks and references to Appendices
night 26/27 July	26/7/16	11.15pm	Operation in conjunction with Infantry.	AMS
		11.17pm	Gas alert received from B/187.	
		11.30pm	Gas reported coming over by D/187.	
			A/187 and D/187 report no signs of gas.	
	27/7/16	11.0 pm 12.0 m 12.15am	Batteries commenced firing as per schedule. Bombarded enemy's front line trench. Still in communication by telephone with Gap 7, and received report that Infantry, 10th Bn "Queens" Liaison Officer reported Infantry had been over 25 minutes. Note particularly that no flares had been sent up by enemy. The artillery wire were the only wires which held during the operation. Message received from O.C. Enterprise to cease fire.	OMS OMS
		1.5 am	O.C. Enterprise reported that the enemy wire entanglements had been thoroughly well cut by our artillery, and that the front line trench on both flanks had been knocked to pieces by artillery. As soon as our bombardment lifted, the enemy placed a heavy barrage on Infantry front line trench and "no man's land". Identifications obtained proved that the trench was held by the 104th Regiment. Screen, and a machine Gun Coy. (normal) Artillery casualties nil.	
	28/7/16	—	The screen at U.26.d.5.2. reported to have attracted enemy shell fire, and would appear to have attained its purpose. Other screens have not up to the present attracted hostile shelling.	OMS

Army Form C. 2118

WAR DIARY
or
INTELLIGENCE SUMMARY

187th Brigade R.F.A. VOL 4

August 1916.

(Erase heading not required.)

Instructions regarding War Diaries and Intelligence Summaries are contained in F. S. Regs., Part II. and the Staff Manual respectively. Title Pages will be prepared in manuscript.

Place	Date	Hour	Summary of Events and Information	Remarks and references to Appendices
NIEPPE	1/8/16	—	From 11.0 am until 5.0 pm all telephonic communication forward of Brigade Headquarters was suspended in order to test the efficiency of visual signalling. Communication with Batteries was satisfactorily maintained by means of heliograph and lamps.	J.H. Mitchell Capt RFA
	night 2/3rd		Road shoot carried out on area, PONT ROUGE to U.17.d.2½.6½, and AU CHASSEUR CABARET to U.17.d.2.6.6. 512 rounds fired. Retaliation slight. No casualties or damage to material.	J.H. Mitchell Capt RFA
	night 6/7		Enemy "dumps" engaged by B, C & D Batteries. Targets U.22.a.9.8. and U.2.2.c.9.7. Batteries fired in two bursts of 90 rounds each. Retaliation normal. Casualties nil.	J.H. Mitchell Capt RFA
	8/8/16	9.0am to 6.0pm	All telephonic communication forward of Brigade Headquarters again suspended in order to test the efficiency of visual signalling. Communication satisfactorily maintained by means of heliograph and lamps. During this suspension B/187 carried out registration on U.29.b.2.7. HOUSE in PONT ROUGE very effectively.	J.H. Mitchell Capt RFA
	night 8/9th Aug		Road shoot carried out by A/187, B/187, C/187 and B/183. Ground covered PONT ROUGE to U.17.d.2½.6½, and AU CHASSEUR CABARET to U.17.d.2½.6½. No retaliation. Casualties nil.	J.H. Mitchell Capt RFA
	August 20 ('16)	8.0pm	Relief by 106th Brigade R.F.A. completed and Command handed over.	J.H. Mitchell Capt RFA
	21/8/16	6.0am	Brigade vacated position and moved to GODEWAERSVELDE, where it arrived at 12.0 noon.	J.H. Mitchell Capt RFA
	night 23/24th	4.0 pm 4.0 am	Batteries and Headquarter Staff, at 3 hour intervals entrained for ABBEVILLE. They arrived during morning of 24th August. Marched from ABBEVILLE to PONT REMY, where they occupied billets. More satisfactorily carried out, and no accidents.	
			Reason for move is in order that the Brigade should average short training in open warfare, including further training in visual signalling, and alternative means of communication other than by telephone.	J.H. Mitchell Capt RFA

Army Form C. 2118

WAR DIARY
or
INTELLIGENCE SUMMARY 187th Brigade R.F.A.
(Erase heading not required.)

August 1916.

Place	Date	Hour	Summary of Events and Information	Remarks and references to Appendices
PONT REMY	29/8/16	5.0 am	Officer Commanding 187th Brigade R.F.A., together with O.s.C. "A" and "B" Battery and 1 Subaltern from each Battery, proceeded to view the battle in the Somme, under instructions from 41st Divisional Artillery Headquarters.	J.M. Mitchell Lt. RFA
do.	30/8/16	11.30 pm	Received orders that Divisional Artillery would move following evening. Further details later.	J.M. Mitchell Lt. RFA
do.	31/8/16	—	Further instructions received that the Brigade would leave PONT REMY by road at 7.30 pm. 187th Brigade R.F.A. duly departed according for the neighbourhood of DERNACOURT to schedule	J.M. Mitchell Lt. RFA

Army Form C. 2118

WAR DIARY
or
INTELLIGENCE SUMMARY
(Erase heading not required.)

September, 1916.

187th Brigade R.F.A.
VOL 5

41

Instructions regarding War Diaries and Intelligence Summaries are contained in F. S. Regs., Part II. and the Staff Manual respectively. Title Pages will be prepared in manuscript.

Place	Date	Hour	Summary of Events and Information	Remarks and references to Appendices
PONT REMY	1/9/16	7.30pm	The Brigade left PONT REMY on route for ALBERT area. Marched during the night 1/2 September 1916. No mishaps or casualties.	THB
AILLY sur SOMME	2/9/16	4.0am	Arrived at AILLY sur SOMME, where the Brigade rested until 8.30 pm.	THB
		8.30pm	Re-commenced march by road, arriving at Dernancourt at 6.30 am 3/9/16.	
DERNANCOURT	3/9/16	6.30am	Arrived at Dernancourt	THB
"	5/9/16	—	Instructions received that Brigade will go into action on the 7th inst.	THB
"	7/9/16	—	Brigade left DERNANCOURT, Batteries moving off at one hour interval. "A" Battery moved off 10.0 am. Brigade Headquarters left Cart at 2.0 pm. Batteries took up positions as follows:-	THB
			"A" S. 16. d. 2. 3.	
			"B" S. 16. d. 1. 4. } Map reference LONGUEVAL	
			"C" S. 16. c. 7. 4. } 57 c. S.W. 3.	
			"D" S. 22. a. 4. 7.	
"	7/9/16 to 12/9/16		Batteries were engaged in registration etc.	THB

Army Form C. 2118

WAR DIARY
or
INTELLIGENCE SUMMARY

September 1916   187th Brigade R.F.A.

(Erase heading not required.)

Place	Date	Hour	Summary of Events and Information	Remarks and references to Appendices
Position as given above.	13th Sept	-	The preliminary bombardment for the attack to be made on the 15th., began, and was carried on continuously until the morning of the 15th.	T.W.S
	15th	-	An attack on FLERS was made. In the evening all batteries were advanced to a position about S. 11. c. central., and Headquarters advanced to a position about S.16. d. 2. 3. Major Stafford and Lieut. J.P.M. Carpenter killed, and three officers wounded.	T.W.S
S.11.c.	16th to 25th	-	Batteries were engaged in almost continuous bombardment. Captain J.R. Homan wounded 15/9/16.	T.W.S
"	25th	-	This Brigade took part in a successful attack on the village of GUEUDECOURT, in conjunction in 55th Division.	T.W.S

1875 Wt. W593/826 1,000,000 4/15 J.B.C. & A. A.D.S.S./Forms/C. 2118.

Army Form C. 2118

WAR DIARY
or
INTELLIGENCE SUMMARY
(Erase heading not required.)

Instructions regarding War Diaries and Intelligence Summaries are contained in F. S. Regs., Part II. and the Staff Manual respectively. Title Pages will be prepared in manuscript.

Place	Date	Hour	Summary of Events and Information	Remarks and references to Appendices
S.11.b.	27th		The Brigade took part in an attack on portions of GIRD TRENCH which were still in the enemy's hands.	TM10
	28th to 30th		Unusually quiet.	TM10

1875   W. W593/826   1,000,000   4/15   J.B.C. & A.   A.D.S.S./Forms/C. 2118.

Army Form C. 2118

187th Brigade R.F.A.
October 1916. Vol 6

WAR DIARY
or
INTELLIGENCE SUMMARY
(Erase heading not required.)

Instructions regarding War Diaries and Intelligence Summaries are contained in F. S. Regs., Part II. and the Staff Manual respectively. Title Pages will be prepared in manuscript.

Place	Date	Hour	Summary of Events and Information	Remarks and references to Appendices
S.16.c.2.2.	1st.		Batteries occupied positions at about S.11.d, central, and Brigade Headquarters at S.16.c.2.2. Reference map LONGUEVAL 57.c.S.W.3.	JAD
	1st.	4.0am	Fourth Army in conjunction with Reserve Army continued the attack. 187th Brigade R.F.A. took part in the creeping and stationary barrage.	JAD
	2nd to 5th		Brigade actively engaged in registering. Normal day and night shooting carried out. Operation which had been ordered by 41st Div. Arty. Operation Order No. 22 to take place on the 1st and 5th., were postponed until the 6th and 7th.	JAD
	6th.	3.15pm to 5.0pm	The Brigade was engaged in bombardment of enemy trenches in accordance with 41st. Div. Arty. Operation Order No. 22.	JAD
		5.0pm to 7.45am	Bombardment continued at a reduced rate. At zero 12th. Division continued the attack, with 41st Division on left, and 20th Division on right. 41st Divisional Artillery Group took part in the barrage in accordance with Divisional Artillery Operation Order No. 23.	JAD
		8.0pm	Barrage ceased, and normal night firing began.	JAD
	8th.		Officer commanding the Brigade, Lieut: Colonel A.E.M. Stead reported sick, and Major H.W. Hutton R.F.A. assumed command temporarily.	JAD
		2.35pm	Slow bombardment was ordered to be continued throughout the day. Arrangements were made for mutual defence in the case of an attack on our left. and	JAD

WAR DIARY or INTELLIGENCE SUMMARY

187th Brigade R.F.A.
October 1916.

Army Form C. 2118

(Erase heading not required.)

Place	Date	Hour	Summary of Events and Information	Remarks and references to Appendices
			and whichever the Brigade was to shoot on advance of the S.O.S. line on the left half of Divisional Artillery group zone.	J.M.D.
	10/11th.		During the night the 41st Division less Divisional Artillery was relieved by 30th Division.	J.M.D.
	11th.	7.0 am to 5.0 pm	The Brigade took part in a bombardment on enemy trenches, engaging that portion of BAYONET TRENCH in the Brigade zone, in accordance with 41st D.A., O.O. No. 24.	J.M.D.
		5.0 pm to	Bombardment was continued at a reduced rate.	J.M.D.
	12th	7.0 am		J.M.D.
		7.0 am to 2.5 pm	Bombardment was continued at an increased rate.	
			Fourth Army continued the attack, 6th French Army also attacking. XVII Corps attacked with 12th Division on the right and 30th Division on the left. This Brigade took part in the barrage in accordance with 41st. D.A., O.O. No. 25. D/187 took part in a gas barrage.	J.M.D.
		8.30 pm	Barrage discontinued, and normal night firing resumed.	J.M.D.
	13th.	7.0 am	Normal day firing commenced.	J.M.D.

WAR DIARY or INTELLIGENCE SUMMARY

187th Brigade R.F.A.
October 1916.

Army Form C. 2118

Place	Date	Hour	Summary of Events and Information	Remarks and references to Appendices
	13/14 14/15		During these two nights 21st Divisional Artillery was withdrawn and 29th Divisional Artillery came into the line.	JMD
	14th		The Brigade cooperated with the Heavy Artillery in a bombardment of BAYONET TRENCH in accordance with 41st D.A. O.O. No. 26.	JMD
	15th		The 18th Infantry Brigade assaulted part of MILD Trench and other trenches in the enemy's hands. 41st Divisional Artillery cooperated with a creeping barrage in which this Brigade took part, in accordance with 41st D.A.O.O. No. 27.	JMD
			The Brigade also took part in a bombardment of enemy trenches in accordance with 41st D.A.O.O. No. 28.	JMD
			General orders were received that operations would continue on the 18th October, and that all wire on the Brigade front was to be cut.	JMD
			All batteries not engaged in bombardment took part in the wire cutting.	JMD
	16th		Lieut. L.R.P. Shirdon of "A" Battery 187th Brigade R.F.A. carried out a reconnaissance on front line trenches of the enemy wire.	JMD
	15th & 16th		The Brigade cooperated with the Heavy Artillery in an intermittent bombardment of BAYONET TRENCH and LIME TRENCH during the nights 15/16 and 16/17 Oct in accordance with 41st D.A. O.O. No. 29.	JMD

189th Brigade R.F.A. Army Form C. 2118

WAR DIARY
or
INTELLIGENCE SUMMARY
(Erase heading not required.)

October 1916.

Place	Date	Hour	Summary of Events and Information	Remarks and references to Appendices
	17th		Lieut Windsor again visited the front line trenches, and ranged all batteries on enemy wire.	T.M.D.
			Major H.M. Ballingall R.F.A. reported and assumed command of the Brigade, Major H.H. Aulton taking over command of "A" Battery.	T.M.D.
	18th		Fourth Army renewed the attack in conjunction with 6th French Army. 12th Division attacked with 6th Division on the right, and 30th Division on the left. Zero hour 3.40 am. The Brigade cooperated in the barrage, in accordance with Hist D.A.O.O. No. 81, Appendix "A".	T.M.D.
		7.40 am	Orders were received to cease barrage, and a steady rate of fire was maintained on Bayonet Trench in the Brigade Zone and on dead ground and sunken roads to the north. This was continued throughout the day.	T.M.D.
	19th		Orders having been received to reconnoitre positions for the Brigade East of Longueval and FLERS, a reconnaissance was carried out by Major Ballingall and Colonel Sherbrook in cooperation, and a report was made to the Division. Normal shooting was carried out throughout the day.	T.M.D.
	night 19/20		29th Division relieved 12th Division. 41st Divisional Artillery placed under command of G.O.C. 29th Division on completion of relief.	T.M.D.

5.

187th Brigade R.F.A. Army Form C. 2118

WAR DIARY
or
INTELLIGENCE SUMMARY
(Erase heading not required.)

October 1916.

Place	Date	Hour	Summary of Events and Information	Remarks and references to Appendices
	20th 21st 22nd		Normal day and night shooting was carried out.	JNB
	23rd to 28th		Normal day and night shooting was carried out. Operations which should have taken place on the 28th inst., were postponed until 30th, and again until November 1st, 1916.	JNB

Instructions regarding War Diaries and Intelligence Summaries are contained in F. S. Regs., Part II. and the Staff Manual respectively. Title Pages will be prepared in manuscript.

1875. Wt. W593/826 1,000,000 4/15 J.B.C. & A. A.D.S.S./Forms/C. 2118.

187th Brigade R.F.A.
November 1916.

Army Form C. 2118

WAR DIARY
or
INTELLIGENCE SUMMARY
(Erase heading not required.)

Vol 7

Place	Date	Hour	Summary of Events and Information	Remarks and references to Appendices
DERNANCOURT	1/11/16		187th Brigade R.F.A. left Brigade wagon lines and marched to LA NEUVELLE, arriving at 3:30 pm. Remained here until the 3rd inst., in order to rest men and horses, who were in an exhausted condition after leaving the SOMME area.	In extracts
	3/11/16		Brigade left LA NEUVELLE at 7.45 am, and marched to TALMAS, arriving there at 2.30 p.m., and went into billets.	
	4/11/16		Marched to AMPLIER, and billeted there for the night.	In extracts
	5/11/16		Brigade left AMPLIER and marched to CONCHY SUR CANCHE, and billeted there for the night.	In extracts
	6/11/16		Left CONCHY SUR CANCHE and marched to MONCHY CAYEUX, where the Brigade was billeted until the morning of the 9th. November 1916.	In extracts
	9/11/16		Left MONCHY CAYEUX and marched to MOLINGHEM. Billeted for the night.	In extracts
	10/11/16		Brigade marched to HONDEGHEM. Billeted for the night.	In extracts
	11/11/16		Left HONDEGHEM, and marched to BOESCHEPE.	In extracts
	12/11/16		Brigade remained at BOESCHEPE, but one section each of "B" and "C" Batteries 187th Brigade R.F.A. took over from 12th Australian Field Artillery Brigade at H.35.c.1.5.	In extracts

WAR DIARY

187th Brigade R.F.A.

INTELLIGENCE SUMMARY November 1916.

Army Form C. 2118

Place	Date	Hour	Summary of Events and Information	Remarks and references to Appendices
	13/11/16		Remainder of Brigade took over from 12th. Australian Field Artillery Brigade, in position as follows:- H.Q. H.28.a.5.0. "A" Battery At wagon line. "B" " One section at H.34.e.3.3, & one section N.4.a.5.9. "C" " H.35.c.1.5. "D" " at wagon line. The Batteries in action were under the Command of DISPENDAAL GROUP (190th Brigade R.F.A.)	To C/Stunts
	25th to 26th		Batteries took up positions as follows:- "A" Battery. 4 guns at H.29.c.5.7, and 2 guns at H.29.d.5.5. "B" " 4 guns at H.35.B.7.5, and 2 guns at H.29.d.6.5. "C" " 4 guns at H.36.d.0.6, and 2 guns at H.36.d.3½.7. "D" " 4-4.5" Hows at H.30.a.7.8.	To C/Stunts.

WAR DIARY
or
INTELLIGENCE SUMMARY

187th. Brigade R.F.A.
November 1916.

Place	Date	Hour	Summary of Events and Information	Remarks and references to Appendices
	30/11/16		The reorganization of the Brigade was completed. It is now composed of 3 – 6 gun 18 Pdr. Q.F. Batteries, and 1 – 4 – 4.5" Howitzer Battery. A/187 took the Right half of A/183. B/187 took over the Left half of A/183. C/187 took over the Right half of C/183.	To Church

WAR DIARY

187th Brigade R.F.A.
DECEMBER 1916.

INTELLIGENCE SUMMARY

Army Form C. 2118

Place	Date	Hour	Summary of Events and Information	Remarks and references to Appendices
DICKEBUSCH.	1/12/16.		Normal day and night firing carried out.	JM.
	2/12/16		ST ELOI GROUP ARTILLERY in conjunction with 41st Division Infantry, in accordance with 41st Divisional Artillery Operation Order No. 39½, cooperated in carrying out a raid on enemy trenches. DIEPENDAAL ARTILLERY GROUP, 16th Divisional Artillery and 10th Corps H.A., also assisted. This raid was successfully carried. No casualties.	JM.
	3rd to 9th		Normal day and night firing carried out.	JM.
	10/12/16	1.45pm	ST ELOI ARTILLERY GROUP assisted in a Divisional shoot. Batteries taking part were D/187, 1 Belgian Battery. Intention was to destroy enemy front line trenches, as it was suspected he intended making a raid from that point. Positions bombarded were from O.7.b.0.0½ to O.7.b.7.5. This was successfully carried out, much damage being done. Casualties nil. 1 Trench Mortar Battery, D/190, and A/189, also participated.	JM.
	11/12/16	6.0pm	In accordance with 41st Divisional Artillery Operation Order No. 43, Howitzers and 18 Pdr Batteries took part in a ROAD Shoot. Intention:- To bombard certain localities and chief entry lines of communication, thus stopping the traffic causing a block and congestion. When the road is full, it will be subjected to a rapid and heavy bombardment. Batteries in this group taking part A, B, C & D/187, D/190 and Belgian Group. This operation was fully carried out. Casualties nil.	JM.

WAR DIARY or INTELLIGENCE SUMMARY

189th Brigade R.F.A.

DECEMBER 1916.

Army Form C. 2118

Place	Date	Hour	Summary of Events and Information	Remarks and references to Appendices
	14/12/16		A raid was attempted on our left by the enemy, and St Eloi Group was called upon to cooperate. C/187 & Nos. 2 & 3 Belgian Batteries ordered to open slow rate of fire on S.O.S. lines.	J.M.
		9.36pm	1 Belgian Battery ordered to fire from CROONAERT CHAPEL to O.7.c.O.7.	J.M.
		9.42pm	C/187 ordered to stop.	J.M.
		9.43pm	Belgians ordered to double rate of fire.	J.M.
		9.47pm	Ordered A/187 to burst as far right as possible and concentrate on support line, one round per gun per minute.	J.M.
		9.51pm	Stopped.	J.M.
		9.53pm	Cooperate 2 ordered. (41st Divisional Artillery Defence Scheme.)	J.M.
		9.57pm	Batteries reported opened fire.	J.M.
		9.59pm	Double rate of Belgian fire.	J.M.
		10.32pm	Slacken Belgian fire. 1 round per gun per 2 minutes.	J.M.
		10.39pm	" " " " " 4 "	J.M.
		10.47pm	Stop. Stand by.	J.M.
	15/12/16		Normal firing.	J.M.
	16/12/16	1.0 pm	In accordance with 41st Divisional Artillery Operation Order No. 44, a bombardment of enemy front line system was carried out in conjunction with DIEPENDAAL Artillery Group, and MEDIUM TRENCH MORTARS, and HEAVY ARTILLERY.	J.M.

WAR DIARY or INTELLIGENCE SUMMARY

187th Brigade R.F.A.
DECEMBER 1916
Army Form C. 2118

Place	Date	Hour	Summary of Events and Information	Remarks and references to Appendices
	17th to 24th		Localities shelled were, the neighbourhood of HILL 60, and Trenches EAST of the BLUFF, from I.35.a.60.85 to I.29.c.93.26. Normal day and night firing.	J.M.D. J.M.D.
	25/12/16	10:45am	In accordance with 41st Divisional Artillery Operation Order No. 45, a Divisional shoot was carried out. Intention :- To damage new work of the enemy at the following points O.4.d.17, N.18.b.2.9, O.7.b.4.4, O.8.d.7½.2. Batteries taking part A/187, B/187, D/187 and D/190. This operation was duly carried out. Casualties nil. Enemy retaliated somewhat during the afternoon.	J.M.D.
	27/12/16	12 noon to 12.25 pm	In accordance with 41st Divisional Artillery Operation Order No. 47, ST ELOI ARTILLERY GROUP gave a covering fire for a TRENCH MORTAR Bombardment. Batteries taking part A, B, and C/187, shooting at enemy support Trenches as follows :- A/187 --- O.4.a.4½. 3¾. to O.4.c.1½. 2. B/187 --- O.4.a.8. 5. to O.4.a.4½. 3¾. C/187 --- O.8.a.3. 7. to O.2.c.6. 0.	J.M.D.
			Operation successful. Enemy retaliated during the afternoon. Casualties, 2 O.R. wounded, and one of A/187 gun received a direct hit, putting it out of action.	J.M.D.

187th. Brigade R.F.A.

Army Form C. 2118

WAR DIARY
or
INTELLIGENCE SUMMARY
(Erase heading not required.)

DECEMBER 1916

Place	Date	Hour	Summary of Events and Information	Remarks and references to Appendices
	30/12/16	11.45 p.m.	In accordance with 41st. Divisional Artillery Operation Order No. 46, ST ELOI ARTILLERY GROUP took part in a bombardment. Intention :- Bombard hostile Trench mortars about O.7.d. 25, 65, N.19.b.95, 80, O.7.c. 40, 40, and O.7.c. 97, 87. Guns taking part, 2 Howitzers of D/190, shooting on O.7.d. 25, 65, and 3 guns of A/187 giving covering fire on O.7.a. 9½, 1½, to O.7.c. 3½, 5. In order to draw the fire of hostile Trench mortars before the Artillery shoot, the 122nd Trench Mortar Battery arranged for Stokes guns to fire at 1.25 p.m. This operation was carried without any casualties, although hostile aircraft were more active than usual during the shoot. There was slight retaliation during the afternoon, principally on A/187 position.	C
	31/12/16	3.0 pm to 3.30 pm	In accordance with 41st Divisional Artillery Operation Order No. 48, the Brigade cooperated with Trench mortars in wire cutting. B/187 shooting on the support trench system from O.4.a. 1½, 2 to O.4.a. 3½, 4, and from O.4.a. 5, 5, to O.4.a. 8, 5½. No casualties.	J.N.D. J.N.D.

WAR DIARY
or
INTELLIGENCE SUMMARY
(Erase heading not required.)

151 Bde R.F.A.
Army Form C. 2118

Place	Date	Hour	Summary of Events and Information	Remarks and references to Appendices
ST. ELOI	1/4/17		Nothing to report.	
"	2.4.17		Lt. Col. SYMONDS goes on leave. Lt.Col. CARDEN. D.S.O. of 190 Brigade takes Company command of the Group.	
"	3.4.17	9.0 p.m – 9.30 p.m	Covering fire for Trench Mortars during wire cutting operation.	
"	4.4.17	9.30 p.m – 9.55 p.m	" " " " "	
"	5.4.17	10.0 p.m – 10.25 p.m	" " " " "	
"	6.4.17	9.0 p.m – 9.25 p.m	Covering fire for Trench Mortars. Two 18 pdr batteries of 190th Brigade, 1 How. Battery 190th Brigade and 1 How. Battery of 104th A.F.A. Brigade. assisted to reinforce Group in connection with 41st D.A. operation Order 64 & 47th D.A. operation Order No. 21.	Appendix I 41st DA. OO.64 47th DA. OO. 21.
"	"		Expended on wire cutting covering fire on Enemy ammunition dumps. 1600 A.X. 330 B.X. 3", 4.5, 5" & 6" – 100 M.T.M. Bombs.	
"	"	11.30 a.m	Bombardment of DAMM STRASSE by 4.5 how batteries in conjunction with IX & Corps Heavy Artillery, vide 41st DA. operation Order 65	Appendix II 41st DA. OO.65

Army Form C. 2118

WAR DIARY
or
INTELLIGENCE SUMMARY
(Erase heading not required.)

Instructions regarding War Diaries and Intelligence Summaries are contained in F.S. Regs., Part II. and the Staff Manual respectively. Title Pages will be prepared in manuscript.

Place	Date	Hour	Summary of Events and Information	Remarks and references to Appendices
ST. ELOI	7.4.17		Operations in accordance with 41st DA.O.O. 64.	
	8.4.17		Reinforcing batteries leave. Lt.Col. CARDEN hand over to command of Group to 2/Major H.H. HARFORD (County 8/10/7).	
	9.4.17		Nothing to report.	
	10.4.17			
	11.4.17		Two Guns of B/167 relieved by 2 guns of A/104 on left Battalion subsector being handed over to 47th Division.	
	12.4.17		Relief of B/167 by A/104 completed. B/167 remains at Inger Lines.	
	13.4.17		Nil.	
	14.4.17		Nil.	
	15.4.17		Reinforcing batteries assist in connection with proposed raid by 19th Division on HOLLANDSCHESCHUR SALIENT.	
	16.4.17		Proposed raid cancelled. Reinforcing batteries leave.	

1875 Wt. W593/826 1,000,000 4/15 J.B.C. & A. A.D.S.S./Forms/C. 2118.

Army Form C. 2118

WAR DIARY
or
INTELLIGENCE SUMMARY
(Erase heading not required.)

Instructions regarding War Diaries and Intelligence Summaries are contained in F.S. Regs., Part II. and the Staff Manual respectively. Title Pages will be prepared in manuscript.

Place	Date	Hour	Summary of Events and Information	Remarks and references to Appendices
ST. ELOI.	17.4.17 18.4.17 19.4.17		Nil.	See Appendices III, IV, V & VI
	20.4.17	9.0 p.m.	Raid by enemy on Right Battalion subsector. Two attempts to enter trenches on Left Battalion were stopped by our artillery. Fire	
	21.4.17		Nil.	
	23.4.17	3.0 p.m.	Group Shoot on enemy's front line, support & communication trenches. Ammunition expended 500 A.X., 150 B.X. Shrapnel (Belgian) 400.	
	23.4.17		C Battery heavily shelled during the day. Orders by C.R.A. to move guns. 4 guns moved during night 23/24th to H30 a.1.5. 2 guns to horses H3q.b.110.	
	24.4.17		Nil.	
	25.4.17		A & D Batteries heavily shelled. 5 killed. Both positions vacated for some hours.	
	26.4.17		B/187 relieved C/187 during night 25th/26th.	

Army Form C. 2118

WAR DIARY
or
INTELLIGENCE SUMMARY
(Erase heading not required.)

Place	Date	Hour	Summary of Events and Information	Remarks and references to Appendices
ST. ELOI.	26.4.17.		C/187 proceed to RECQUES area to Train with 122nd Infantry Brigade.	
		4.15 - 4.35 a.m.	Covering fire for Trench Mortars during wire-cutting operations.	
			B/187's detached section shelled + most of horses at M.29.c.6.3. Main position also shelled + needed for some hours during the evening.	
	27.4.17	6.30 & 6.50 p.m.	Covering fire for Trench Mortars.	
	28.4.17	4.0 - 4.30 p.m.	Covering fire for Trench Mortars.	
	29.4.17	3 p.m.	Group Shoot on houses O.14.d. 26.4.43 believed to be opening used as billets. 350 6.X. 150 H.E. 200 Shrapnel (Belgian) expended.	
	30.4.17	6.0 pm - 6.20 pm	Covering fire for Trench Mortars	
		5.15 & 5.35 pm	Covering fire for Trench Mortars.	

Lieut. Colonel R.S.A.
Commanding 187th Brigade R.S.A.

H936.

WAR DIARY OF 187th. BRIGADE R.F.A. FOR MARCH 1917.

March 1st.)
    to   ) Brigade in rest at RYVELD near CASSEL.
March 14th.)

Night of
March 15/16th. Relieved 189th. Brigade R.F.A. in the St. Eloi Sector from O.4.a. to O.1.d. (sheet 28 S.W.), 190th. Brigade R.F.A. holding the sector on our right and a Brigade of the 47th. Division that on our left.
Three Batteries of the 13th. Belgian Artillery Group attached for tactical purposes.

March 16th.)
    to   ) Hostile Artillery very active during this period on
March 23rd.) back areas -"CHATEAU SEGARD","CAFE BELGE","DICKEBUSCH ROAD", "ELSENWALLE" etc., using a considerable amount of gas shell.
Our Artillery normal.

March 24th. At 7.30 p.m. after an intense bombardment by Trench Mortars and Artillery, a small party of the enemy (8 men) entered our trenches in O.4.a. (sheet 28 S.W.) about 200 yards South of the YPRES-COMINES CANAL.
Our casualties were not heavy and no men were missing.
It is thought that our Artillery inflicted serious losses on the enemy as he assembled for the raid, and that the raiding party would have been larger but for effectiveness of our barrage.
This raid took place simultaneously with a raid on the BLUFF CRATER and the blowing up of a small mine in the HILL 60 SECTOR.

March 25th.)
    to   ) Considerable hostile shelling on back areas. Our
March 31st.) artillery normal.

During the month the only casualties from hostile shell fire were one officer (gassed) and two Other Ranks.

Lieut. Colonel R.F.A.
Commanding St Eloi Artillery Group.

April 27th. 1917.

WAR DIARY or INTELLIGENCE SUMMARY

Army Form C. 2118

187 Bde R.F.A.
WD / 3

MAY 1917

Place	Date	Hour	Summary of Events and Information	Remarks and references to Appendices
BUCQUOY	1/5, 2/5	9 p.m.	Produces barrage in conjunction with 47 F.A. D.A.	Scene with fire guards [Appendix I]
	3/4/5		Half batteries of A/187, B/187 + D/187 relieved by A/190, C/190 + D/190. Relief of A.C + D batteries completed. Right & half batteries from Dickebusch to LA CYTÉ. W.W. at 9 a.m. Bde H.Q.rs	
	4/5		to in Capt Rosevi.	
LA CYTÉ from 5/5/17	5/5/17		A.C + D batteries employed in building battery positions in connection with X scheme.	
			11 cm Spanish Hows in charge of [?] troughts + stores? conveniation to all X scheme positions. Establishment 1200 lb.s per gun 18 pdr + 1100 rounds per 4.5 How.	
			9. 18 pdr batteries 0 + 4.5 How batteries completed to short establishment in minus 1 Light howitzer. 2000 rounds	

Army Form C. 2118

WAR DIARY
or
INTELLIGENCE SUMMARY
(Erase heading not required.)

Instructions regarding War Diaries and Intelligence Summaries are contained in F. S. Regs, Part II. and the Staff Manual respectively. Title Pages will be prepared in manuscript.

Place	Date	Hour	Summary of Events and Information	Remarks and references to Appendices
LA CLYTTE	7641 May	9.10 p.m.	enemy commenced [?] a heavy bombardment of Eighth Lines (H=29 d Sheet 28). 2./1 B/17 batteries + 1 Gun Sec. Battery filled Y bombardment. + stretcher at Bampfeler 10 officer + other ranks wounded.	
	10/11/15		A/17 wagon line shelter. 14 horses killed.	
			Half B/17 moved to position at Nieu S B (Sheet 28) to Nieuport. Group is only to fire in case of S.O.S.	
	11/12		Move of B/17 into action completed.	
	19 th		C/17 return from Newp'f, start work in position to the [?] of [?] in connection with X scheme.	
	28 th		Capt d L Symonds [?] Lt Col Symonds takes command of Northern Artillery Group, consisting of 187 Bde [?] + D/27 (known as C Group) and [?]	

1875 Wt. W593/826 1,000,000 4/15 J.B.C. & A. A.D.S.S./Forms/C. 2118.

Army Form C. 2118

WAR DIARY
or
INTELLIGENCE SUMMARY
(Erase heading not required.)

Instructions regarding War Diaries and Intelligence Summaries are contained in F.S. Regs., Part II. and the Staff Manual respectively. Title Pages will be prepared in manuscript.

Place	Date	Hour	Summary of Events and Information	Remarks and references to Appendices
DICKEBUSCH	28th		A/52 Brigade headquarters move to Dickebusch (H34b3.7). The howitzers of 28th A.B. & D batteries came into action respectively in squares H29c, H29d & H35b.	Appendix II
				Appendix III
	29th		Night firing on in sqd DA 52194	
			" " " " " " 52223	Appendix IV
			In action C/187 move to posh in N6a in accordance with Art DA 0.0.71.	Appendix V
	30th	11.30am	Positive board n- 411 DA 52229.	
			Howitzer 2 section J C/187 move into action Art DA 52238	Appendix VI
			Night firing on Art DA 0.0.82	Appendix VII
	31st		Night firing on 0.0.82	

Signed [signature]
Lieutenant Colonel R.A.
Commanding 187th Brigade R.F.A.

41st Division

Diary of
187 Bde R.F.A.
for June '17
is missing

disposal of Voivode Bojović, commanding the First Army. The German counter-plan was that the Austrian 9th Division, joined by the German troops of the LXI Corps, should delay the advance as long as possible on the line Priština - Vranje and cover the detrainment and deployment of the other reinforcing divisions in its rear. The German remnants of the LXII Corps, if they could not break out through Skoplje, were to make their way over the mountains through Pristina to Niš. The roads and railways to the north were all clear — General von Scholtz had seen to that. He had had all Bulgarian columns and stragglers reaching Kumanovo turned east in the direction of Kyustendil so that they should not choke the Southern Morava corridor and prevent the escape of his Germans.

The energy with which the First Army of Voivode Bojovic threw itself upon the Austrian 9th Division, and the indifferent resistance of the latter, upset the German plan and brought the Serbians in front of Niš before the detrainment and deployment had been completed. The Serbians made contact with the enemy on the 3rd October, and after a short fight drove him back head-long. The Austrian division and the German troops of the LXI Corps poured back through the Metarica Pass. The Serbians, now joined by their Cavalry Division, pursued in haste; a rear guard which attempted to hold them up at Leskovac was hustled out of it on the 7th, the French and Serbian

Army Form C. 2118.

187th. BRIGADE, ROYAL FIELD ARTILLERY.

J U L Y, 1917.

WAR DIARY
or
INTELLIGENCE SUMMARY

(Erase heading not required.)

Instructions regarding War Diaries and Intelligence Summaries are contained in F. S. Regs., Part II. and the Staff Manual respectively. Title Pages will be prepared in manuscript.

No. 15

Place	Date	Hour	Summary of Events and Information	Remarks and references to Appendices
DEAD DOG FARM.	1st to 4th.		Brigade in action at positions detailed in Appendix XIV, June War Diary. No Operations of importance.	
	5th.		Brigade relieved by 112 (ARMY) Brigade, Batteries and Headquarters withdrawn to Wagon Lines.	
	6th.		Brigade marches to BOESCHEPE.	
BOESCHEPE.	7th. to 19th.		Brigade resting at BOESCHEPE.	
ST. ELOI.	20th.		Brigade moves into action. Headquarters to DEAD DOG FARM, Batteries to positions marked on attached map.C/104 reinforces Group.	Appendix I.
			Group Zone, (ST.ELOI GROUP) shown on appendix II	Appendix II.
		3 p.m.	S.O.S.Lines until further orders - O.5.a.70.18 - O.11.a.80.05. Night firing.,vide Appendix III.	Appendix III.
			General orders re night firing,vide 41st D.A.Special Instructions No.6.	Appendix IV.
ST.ELOI.	21st.	2 p.m.	S.O.S.Lines O.11.a.80.08 - O.11.a.80.65 divided between 5 18-pdr batteries.Fourth 18-pdr Battery and hows reinforcing on whole front. 60 rounds AX per battery fired by A/187 and B/187 on area between vertical grid lines running through O.11.and O.12.Central,during the day.Night firing as in H.4231.	Appendix V.
	22nd.	9 a.m.	Brigade comes under command of 41st D.A. On 20th and 21st Brigade was under command of 47th D.A.	
		7.5 p.m.	Practice Barrage. O.O.No.1. Night firing on same targets as in Appendix V.	Appendix VI.

Army Form C. 2118.

WAR DIARY
or
INTELLIGENCE SUMMARY
(Erase heading not required.)

Instructions regarding War Diaries and Intelligence Summaries are contained in F. S. Regs., Part II. and the Staff Manual respectively. Title Pages will be prepared in manuscript.

Place	Date	Hour	Summary of Events and Information	Remarks and references to Appendices
ST.ELOI.	23rd.		Day firing on same targets as in Appendix V. Support for raid by 140th Infantry Brigade as in Operation Order No.2.	Appendix VII.
	24th.		Night firing as in Appendix V. Night firing 200 rounds A & AX on area between vertical Grid lines running through 0.11.& 0.12. Central, 80 rounds HX on HOLLEBEKE Cross Roads, 0.12.a. Canal Crossing at 0.12.b. and Track junctions in P.7.a.	
		10 P.M.	Group Headquarters moves from DEAD DOG FARM to H.36.c.3.1.	
	25th.	4 P.M.	Concentrated shoot on P.7.d.15.88, 40 rounds per gun from all guns in Group.	Appendix VIII.
		10.17 P.M.	Shoot with Lethal and smoke shell as in O.O.No.3.	
	26th.		Night firing 250 rounds A & AX on Tracks at 0.12.a.4.9. - Footbridge at 0.12.b. and Canal from 0.12.d.90.65 - P.7.c.00.55. Day firing - 100 rounds A & AX on 0.12.a.53.20 and P.7.c.92.35. Night firing - 250 rounds A & AX on Canal Crossing, Dug-outs and roads - Lock 5 at P.12.b.4.4 bombarded with lethal shell by 4.5" Howitzers from 12.15 a.m. to 12.50 a.m.	
	27th.		Order re resting guns and revised allotment of ammunition received from 41st D.A. (S.2790). 41st D.A.instructions re Liaison and revised allotment of ammunition received (S.2798). Night firing - 130 rounds A & AX on roads. 100 rounds of HX on lock 5, dug-out at 0.12.b.45.32 and Canal Crossing - 0.12.b.2.7.	Appendix X.
	28th.		Day firing - 150 rounds A & AX on suspected machine gun emplacement 0.12.a.53.20 and concrete dug-out at 0.12.d.90.82. Night firing 130 rounds A & AX on roads in 0.12.b. and P.7.a. 100 rounds HX on targets detailed for 27th.	
	29th.		Day firing - 150 rounds A & AX on targets as for 28th. 30 rounds HX on suspected machine gun at 0.12.a.53.20. Allotment of ammunition increased. See 41st D.A.Special Instructions No.S.2809. Night firing 125 rounds A & AX on roads, D/187 on targets as for night firing 28th.	Appendix XI.

Army Form C. 2118.

WAR DIARY
or
INTELLIGENCE SUMMARY
(Erase heading not required.)

Instructions regarding War Diaries and Intelligence Summaries are contained in F. S. Regs., Part II. and the Staff Manual respectively. Title Pages will be prepared in manuscript.

Place	Date	Hour	Summary of Events and Information	Remarks and references to Appendices
ST.ELOI.	30th.		Day firing - 150 rounds A & AX on targets as for 28th, 80 rounds BX on dug-out at P.12.b.45.32	
			Night firing as for 29th.	
			Proposal for attack on WARNETON LINE received from D.A. See H.4581 attached.	Appendix XII.
	31st.	3.50 p.m.	Zero hour for attack in conjunction with 5th Army and the French. Barrage Tables attached, also orders for the advance of batteries to positions in O.9.b in the event of the attack being successful.	Appendix XIII. Appendix XIV.
		3.35 a.m.	Increase rate of fire to 1 round per gun per minute for 15 minutes.	
		1.5 p.m.	S.O.S. reported in front of HOLLEBEKE.	
		1.20 p.m.	All quiet. Half guns ordered to rest, remainder to 1 round per gun per 6 minutes (18-pdrs), 1 round per gun per 8 minutes, 4.5" Howitzers.	

+0+0+0+0+0+0+0+0+0+0+0+0+0+0+0+0+0+0+0+0+0+0+

Lieut;Colonel, R.F.A.
Commanding St. Eloi Artillery Group.

Batty Positions For Offensive

Appendix I.

- B104
- A104 A189
- C189 B189
- BATTLE WOOD
- D189
- H.Qs. BATTLEWOOD D104

- H.Qs. BLUFF
- D47
- D235 BLUFF
- B235 C47 D10AN
- A235 H.Qs. CANAL A10N
- B10AN
- CANAL
- C10AN
- A11AN
- B190 C235 A236
- D190 OOSTHOEK C190 A190 D11AN
- C11AN B236 C236 B11AN
- CHATEAU

- H.Qs. OOSTHOEK
- H.Qs. CHATEAU
- St Eloi

- B47
- A47
- C104 C187
- B187
- ST ELOI
- D187 A187

Appendix II

Group Zones for Offensives

Battle Wood
Bluff
Canal
Chateau
Oosthoek
St Eloi
Hollebeke

NIGHT FIRING 20/21st JULY

REFERENCE:- HOLLEBEKE 1/10.000

German trenches corrected to 29/6/17

Appendix III

A/187 Bursts of fire on crossings over the CANAL at

    O.12.b.7.9)
    Lock No. 5)   Transport Crossings.
    O.6.c.95.10)

    O.12.b.25.65)
    O.12.b.20.75) Footbridges
    O.12.b.05.95)

B/187 Search tracks with one section on each track

    O.6.c.72.70 to O.6.d.0.5
    O.6.c.80.10 to O.6.d.30.25
    O.12.b.50.45 to O.12.b.90.40

D/187 One How. on each of following points:-

    P.7.a.10.30   O.6.d.80.41
    P.7.a.80.40   O.6.b.95.07
    P.7.b.55.20   P.1.c.90.90

Each 18-pr. battery will fire 75 rounds between 10 p.m. and 4 a.m. in bursts of fire at irregular intervals.

4.5" How. battery will fire 125 rounds during the same hours.

20/7/17

                                                Lieut. & Adjt.
                                       St. Eloi Arty. Group.

To: Officer Commanding,
   BLUFF GROUP.

   Reference 47th D.A. Operation Order No. 54 of 18th July 1917, will you please help in this night firing by search with one 18-pr. battery and 75 rounds the following:-

   18-pr. battery.

   Track from O.6.d.81.41 to P.1.c.87.12
   Track from P.1.a.24.09 to P.1.c.91.89

20/7/17

Lieut. Col. RFA
Cmdg. St. Eloi Arty. Group.

SECRET   COPY NO. 9

41st Divisional Artillery Instructions No. 6.

NIGHT FIRING.

Reference Maps. Special HOLLEBEKE.
               Special 8150/1.

                                          17th July 1917.

Principal. 1. With a view to isolating the enemy garrison, night
              firing by 18-pr and 4.5" Hows. will be carried out
           throughout the bombardment.
              The greatest care must be taken that night firing does
           not degenerate into a routine. Unexpected bursts
           of fire are preferable to fire at regular intervals.

Zones   2. The dividing line between the inner and outer zone
              will be the ZANDVOORDE line. The Inner Zone will be dealt
           with by 18-pr, 4.5" How. and Machine Guns.

Tasks.   3. 18-prs will search tracks and roads within their zone
              and will search and sweep their zone boldly with bursts
           to prevent the enemy moving freely over the open country
           clear of the tracks.
              In addition 18-prs are responsible for preventing repairs
           being carried out to works and wire etc in their zone
           damaged by the Heavy Artillery
              4.5" Howitzers will deal with bridges, principal tracks,
           junctions, tramways etc., marked by red circles on attached
           map. From midnight Y/Z night until 4 a.m. Z day, Gas
           Shell if available will be fired by selected 4.5" How.
           Batteries - further orders regarding this will be issued later.

           4. A Map illustrating the latest information as to roads
              and approaches in use is issued herewith.

                                          H.W.L. Waller.
                                                Brigade Major.
           Issued at 10/30am   41st Divisional Artillery.

           To all recipient of Instructions No.5.

From:- Adjutant St Eloi Artillery Group.   H4251

To:- Officers Commanding Batteries.

NIGHT FIRING JULY 21/22nd.

C/187 between dusk and midnight will fire on road running from P.7.c.90.40. to P.7.a.10.32., also on road from P.7.c.60.65. to P.7.c.10.32.

C/104 will fire on the same targets between midnight and dawn.

D/187 will fire on canal crossings - O.12.b.7.0., Lock No.5 and O.12.d.25.65. from ~~midnight~~ dusk till dawn.

Each 18-pdr battery will expend 75 rounds, 25% A and 75% AX. 4.5" Battery will expend 125 rounds BX.

These rounds should be distributed throughout the period, and would suggest they be fired with short bursts of fire by the 18-pdrs at odd intervals, 4.5's keeping these crossings under fire throughout the night.

                                                                Lieut.R.F.A.
                                              Adjutant St Eloi Artillery Group.

July 21st.1917.

H4236

From:- Adjutant St Eloi Artillery Group.

To:- Officer Commanding C/187th. Brigade R.F.A.
     "   "   C/104th. Brigade R.F.A.

Extract from 47th. Intelligence Summary.

"An infantry track from LOCK 5 to dug-outs at O.12.d.3.50 and thence to the trenches in O.18.b. is marked out with small white flags and evidently used at night"

Please expend 20 rounds out of your allotment for tonight at sometime during the specified period, to keep this track under fire at irregular intervals.

Lieut. R.F.A.
Adjutant St Eloi Artillery Group.

July 21st, 1917.

Legend
Principal Roads Used
    "   Tracks "
Gaps in Wire
Tramways Used
Bridges

BATTLE WOOD
BLUFF
CANAL
CHATEAU
OOSTHOEK
ST ELOI

Hollebeke

From:- Adjutant St Eloi Artillery Group.
To:- Officers Commanding Batteries.

Appendix VI   W.D

ST. ELOI ARTILLERY GROUP OPERATION ORDER NO.1

1. A Practice Barrage will be carried out on the 22nd. July in conjunction with the 19th. Division who will at the same time raid the hostile trenches. 41st. Divisional Artillery will assist.

2. ZERO HOUR will be 7.5 p.m.

3. Each Battery will send an officer to Group H.Q. at 5.30 p.m. with a watch to synchronise watches.

4. Os.C. CANAL AND BLUFF Groups are each detailing a Battery Commander to report on the barrage, particularly on the following points :-

    (a) Any gaps in the barrage, particularly in conjunction with flank.
    (b) Short shooting.
    (c) Punctuality of commencement, and lifts etc.
    (d) Accuracy.

5. Rates of fire (a) Creeping Barrage.

    Z to Z plus 4.................. 4 rounds per gun per minute.
    Z plus 4 to Z plus 10......... 3   "   "   "   "   "
    Z plus 10 to Z plus 40........ 1   "   "   "   "   "
    Z plus 40 to "Stop"........... 1   "   "   "   "   "   two minutes.

    (b) Standing Barrage.

    Z to Z plus 15................. 2 rounds per gun per minute.
    Z plus 15 to Z plus 35........ 1   "   "   "   "   "

    (c) 4.5" Howitzers.

    Throughout 1 round per how per minute.

6. Ammunition. Creeping Barrage, 50% AX with Delay.
             Standing Barrage, 75% AX Direct

CREEPING BARRAGE.

    Z to Z plus 4   C/187..... O.11.a.90.65.-O.11.a.66.45.
                         B/187..... O.11.a.86.45.-O.11.a.80.25.
                         A/187..... O.11.a.80.25.-O.11.a.75.10.
    Z plus 4 to Z plus 8 C/187..... O.11.b.20.65.-O.11.b.10.45.
                         B/187..... O.11.b.10.45.-O.11.b.03.26.
                         A/187..... O.11.b.03.26.-O.11.a.90.95.
    Z plus 8 to "Stop"   C/187..... O.11.b.50.65.-O.11.b.38.43.
                         B/187..... O.11.b.38.43.-O.11.b.25.23.
                         A/187..... O.11.b.25.23.-O.11.b.12.03.

STANDING BARRAGE.

    Z to Z plus 15   C/104..... O.11.b.30.62.-O.11.b.02.00.
    Z plus 15 to Z plus 35 C/104.. O.12.a.50.60.-O.12.c.12.95.

4.5" HOWITZERS.

    Z plus 4 to Z plus 20 D/187.. 1 gun on FOREST FARM O.11.b.92.08
                           D/187.. 2 guns on road from O.12.a.00.62.-
                                   O.11.b.68.56.
    Z plus 20 to Z plus 40 D/187.. O.12.b.70.60.-O.12.b.31.40.-
                                   O.12.d.15.95.

July 22nd. 1917.   Joe Cohendin   Lieut. R.F.A.
                                          Adjutant St Eloi Artillery Group.

From:- Adjutant St Eloi Artillery Group.
To:- Officers Commanding Batteries.

Appendix VII

ST ELOI ARTILLERY GROUP OPERATION ORDER NO.2.

1. On the night of the 23/24th. July two raids will be carried out, raid (A) by the 140th. Infantry Brigade who will raid OBLIQUE TRENCH and Wood in O.5.d., raid (B) by 142nd. Infantry Brigade who will raid ruins, trenches and wood in the vicinity of I.36.d.2.3.

2. ST ELOI GROUP will assist in supporting raid (A).

3. ZERO HOUR will be 10.0 p.m.

4. Batteries will send an officer with a watch to Group H.Q. at 6.0 p.m.

5. Artillery Support.

   C/104......... At Zero to Zero plus 5 - O.11.b.30.62., O.11.b.20.30. O.11.b.10.00.
   At Zero plus 5 to Zero plus 30 lift to a line - O.12.a.10.65.-O.10.d.60.95.

   Rates of fire. Zero to Zero plus 4... 4 rounds per gun per minute.
   Zero plus 4 to Zero plus 12... 3 rds per gun per min
   Zero plus 12 to Zero plus 30.. 2 " " " " "
   After Zero plus 30, if required, 1 round per gun per minute.

   Ammunition. Zero to Zero plus 6....... A.
   Zero plus 6 to "Stop".... 60% AX Delay.

   A/187......... At Zero tp Zero plus 5 - 1 section on hostile machine gun at O.11.b.2.6.

   Rates of fire. Zero to Zero plus 5... 4 rounds per gun per minute.

   Ammunition. 50% AX Delay, 50% AX Direct.

   D/187......... At Zero to Zero plus 30 - O.12.a.10.65.-O.10.d.60.95.

   Rate of fire. Zero to Zero plus 30... 1 round per how per minute.

   Ammunition. BX.

6. ACKNOWLEDGE.

Lieut.R.F.A.
Adjutant St Eloi Artillery Group.

July 23rd, 1917.

From:- Adjutant St Eloi Artillery Group.

To:- Officers Commanding Batteries.

AMENDMENT TO OPERATION ORDER NO.2.

Para.5 <u>Rates of fire</u>.

    C/104.... Z to Z plus 4........... 3 rounds per gun per minute.
              Z plus 4 to Z plus 16.. 2   "   "   "   "   "
              Z Plus 16 to Z plus 40. 1   "   "   "   "   "

    D/187   For Zero plus 30 read "Zero plus 40".

                                                    Lieut.R.F.A.
                                        Adjutant St Eloi Artillery Group.

July 23rd.1917.

From:- Adjutant St Eloi Artillery Group.

To:- Officer Commanding D/187.

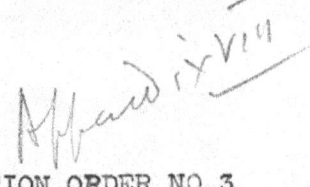

ST ELOI ARTILLERY OPERATION ORDER NO.3

1. On the night of 25/26th. July you will engage the following points with SK, CBR or PS Shell.

2. Zero Hour will be 10.17 p.m.

3. Task allotted to you will be as under :-

   Tram, Road and Track Junction at P.7.b.5.2.

4. Ammunition allotted for task, 42 rounds SK and 150 CBR or PS.

5. Rates of fire and ammunition.

   Z to Z plus 5, 2 rounds per how per min., Lethal, CBR or PS.

   Z plus 5 to
   Z plus 20.   Nothing.

   Z plus 20 to
   Z plus 23.   1 round per how per min., SK.

   Z plus 23 to
   Z plus 43.   Nothing.

   Z plus 43 to
   Z plus 46.   1 round per how per min., SK, CBR or PS., 12 SK
                                                              6 CBR
                                                              or PS.

   Z plus 46 to Z
   plus 66.   Nothing.

   Z plus 66 to
   Z plus 68.   1 round per how per min., SK.

   Z plus 82 to
   Z plus 87.   2 rounds per how per min., CBR or PS.

   Z plus 87 to
   Z plus 102.   Nothing.

   Z plus 102 to
   Z plus 104.   2 rounds per how per min., CBR or PS.

   Total - 42 SK., 150 CBR or PS.

6. ACKNOWLEDGE.

                                            Lieut.R.F.A.
                                    Adjutant St Eloi Artillery Group.

July 25th. 1917.

Appendix IX

S2790

Battle Wood Group
Bluff Group
Canal Group
Chateau Group
Oosthoek Group
St Eloi Group
41st Div. G   )
Xth Corps R.A.) For information.
47th Bde. R.F.A.
104th (Army) Bde. R.F.A.

1. 18-prs up to equivalent of two guns per battery and 4.5" Hows. up to 1 per battery are to be rested until noon 30th July.

   Group Commanders are to select the personnel and guns in their own Groups.

   Where guns are out at I.O.M., they should not be brought in when ready unless strength of Group falls below an average of 4 guns per battery.

2. Under this arrangement Groups will have guns in action and manned as follows:-

Battle Wood Group.	20 18-prs	5, 4.5" Hows.
Bluff Group	20 "	10, "
Canal Group	20 "	5, "
Chateau Group.	16 "	2, "
Oosthoek Group.	16 "	10, "
St Eloi Group.	16 "	5, "

   Guns in excess of this will be withdrawn to wagon lines night 26/27th July, the move being complete by 9 a.m. 27th July.

3. Group Commanders will arrange that no two guns of their Group shall move within 400 yds distance of each other, and not more than two guns per Group per hour from 9 p.m. 26th until 5 a.m. 27th and from 5 to 9 a.m. 27th not more than three guns per hour, 50% must be moved before 5 a.m. 27th inst.

4. Orders will be issued for the return of guns and personnel, this will commence on the night 29/30th July.

5. Ammunition allotment until further orders.

   (a) Night firing 100 rounds per Group.

   (b) By day. Average of 10 rounds per Battery for checking barrage and 20 rounds per Group for general purposes.

   (c) All ammunition required for destroying, and keeping open wire will be in addition to the above.

H W L Waller
Brigade Major
41st Divisional Artillery.

26-7-17.

SECRET Appendix IX X   S2798   COPY NO. 12.

41st DIVL. ARTY. SPECIAL INSTRUCTION No.6.

27th July 1917.

S.O.S. Signal. 1. The S.O.O. Signal for the II Army will be remain as at present, a gold and silver Rain Rocket.
That of the Fifth Army will be a succession of Rifle Rockets each bursting simultaneously into 2 red and 2 Green Lights.

Liaison. 2. (a) With effect from night of 27/28th July until the morning of Y day Liaison Officers with Infantry Battalions in the line from Right to left will be found as under:-

122nd Infantry Bde.) ST ELOI Group
2 Battalions in the line) OOSTHOEK Group.

123rd Infantry Bde.) CANAL Group
3 Battalions in the line) BLUFF GROUP
Battle Wood Group.

(b) R.A. Liaison Officers will arrive at Battalion H.Qrs in sufficient time each evening to make themselves thoroughly conversant with the situation regarding our Infantry Posts, Patrols, etc. They will remain at Battalion H.Qrs until one hour after "Stand to" the following morning.

(c) R.A. Liaison Officers must know the S.O.S. lines of the Group or Groups, covering the Battalion to which he is attached, and their night firing programme.
He must notify the Groups affected of the movements of any of our patrols who might be endangered by night shoots.

(d) There are at present no special Artillery Liaison telephone lines.
Liaison Officers must communicate with the Group or Groups covering the Battalion front - through Infantry lines and Infantry Brigade H.Qrs.
Movements of our patrols must be reported by orderly only.

(e) The present Liaison Officer with Infantry Brigade H.Qrs will be discontinued.

Ammunition 3. Until further orders the ammunition allotment per Group front is as under:-

(a) 18-prs 150 rounds by day including rounds required for checking barrage.
125 rounds by night.

(b) 4.5" Hows. per battery.
By day   50 rounds
By night 100 rounds.
Above is exclusive of ammunition required to cut wire or keep destroyed wire open.

4. (a) Intense Counter-Battery work will be carried out on the 28th and 30th July.
(b) 6" Hows. will engage wire and strong point at I.36.d.20.30 to 20.4/5 with aeroplane on the morning of 27th inst at about 7 a.m. if clear enough.

Hugh Waller.
Brigade Major
41st Divisional Artillery.

26-7-17
Issued at:-
To all recipients of 41st D.A. Special Instructions.

SECRET   Appendix XI   COPY NO. 8

41st D.A., SPECIAL INSTRUCTIONS For 29th JULY 1917

28th JULY 1917

1. Normal day Tasks of searching of shell holes, checking barrage lines, cutting of any undestroyed wire, etc., will be proceeded with.

   Night tasks, as at present, searching of approaches, Tracks, etc., Front line and all destroyed wire to be kept under intermittant bursts of fire.

2. Ammunition allotment is increased as under:-

   (a)   18-pr by day   150 rounds
                by night   200 rounds
   per Group front exclusive of any ammunition required for wirecutting, or keeping destroyed wire open.

   (b)   4.5" Howitzer per Battery by day   80 rounds
                                     by night   120 rounds.

3. The D.T.M.O. will arrange to bombard dugouts and M.G. emplacement at O.6.a.57.67 and O.6.a.52.60. with the two 6" Newton Mortars North of the Canal between 5.50 p.m. and 6.50 p.m.
   Ammunition allotted :-   120 rounds which should not be with "Instantaneous Fuze".

   O.C., Canal Group will arrange for necessary covering fire a special ammunition allotment of 120 rounds 18-prs and 36 rounds 4.5" How. is given for this purpose.

   The D.T.M.O. should make all necessary arrangements direct with O.C., Canal Group (H.Qrs, VICTORIA MINE SHAFT at O.2.a.8.2). O.C. Canal Group will inform G.O.C., 123rd Infantry Brigade of the arrangements made.

                                                     Brigade Major

Issued at: 41st Divisional Artillery.

Copy No. 1   41st Div. G.
"   "   2   R.A. Xth Corps
"   "   3   Battle Wood Group
"   "   4   Bluff Group
"   "   5   Canal Group
"   "   6   Chateau Group
"   "   7   Oosthoek Group
"   "   8   St Eloi Group
"   "   9   D.T.M.O.
"   "   10   41st D.M.G.O.
"   "   11   Lt.Col. Hutchinson.
"   "   12   122nd Inf. Bde.
"   "   13   123rd Inf. Bde.
"   "   14   124th Inf. Bde.
"   "   15   41st D.A. Sigs.
"   "   16   War Diary
"   "   17-20 File

H.4581.

From:- Adjutant St.Eloi Artillery Group.

To:- Officers Commanding Batteries.

In continuation of my H.4540 preliminary notice and suggestions for attack on WARNETON line.

1. The suggested creeping barrage lines should be timed on all maps in lifts of 4 minutes to yellow line, which is reached in Sector I at Z'plus 100 (Z' being the new zero for this attack) in Sector II northern half Z'plus 100, southern half at Z'plus 88 in Sector III the same as II and in Sector I at Z' plus 84.

2. These lifts should be carefully marked in, as it is not known to what depth the attack may be pushed, and consequently to what depth the barrage would be needed. It is of course understood that it would not go beyond the limit marked in yellow, but it might have to check at any lift after Zero'plus 60/64.

3. As a forecast of what might take place, I suggest the following :-

(a) At Zplus 2 (Z being the proper zero hour for the attack on the Red, Blue and Green lines) orders might arrive at R.A.,H.Q., 41st Division to push forward batteries. These orders might arrive at Groups and wagon lines at Z plus 3. First three batteries of Northern and first three batteries of St.Eloi might arrive in positions Z plus 6 followed by two more in each Group to be in position at Z plus 9; all should immediately register on WARNETON line in their new sectors, the F.O.O's having been pushed out ahead of their batteries. Northern Group would probably find O.P's near KLEIN ZILLEBEKE. Some registration should be completed by Z plus 11.

(b) If the above optimistic forecast comes off or seems to be well under way, IXth Corps might sanction an advance of 2 batteries 18-pdrs OOSTHOEK and one battery 18-pdr BATTLE WOOD about Z plus 4. These batteries would be "B" & "C"/190 and B/189. They should be warned of this possibility and would receive orders to harness up at say Z plus 5 from this office. I estimate they would reach their guns at Z plus 7 and arrive at new positions Z plus 10 and commence registration.

(c) About Z plus 10 one might reckon to get some decision as to whether the WARNETON line would be attacked, and an advance might actually commence say Z plus 13 assuming there was sufficient light for the purpose.

4. (a) Artillery action would then be as follows :- New Zero indicated as Z.

STANDING BARRAGE.	Standing Barrage of		
	3 18-pdr Batteries A/235, B/235, C/235. 2 4.5" How. Batteries.	North Group.	WARNETON LINE. Sector 1.
	3 18-pdr Batteries A/104, B/104, C/189. 1 4.5" How Battery.	Battle Wood.	WARNETON LINE. Sector II.
	1 18-pdr Battery. A/47.	Chateau.	}
	2 18-pdr Batteries. B/190 and C/190.	Oosthoek.	}
	3 4.5"How Batteries.	Both above Groups.	}

-2-

5 18-pdr Batteries.	St.Eloi(advanced)	WARNETON LINE.
1 4.5"How.Battery.	-do-	Sector III.

Leaving one 18-pdr Battery ST.ELOI available for "Fleeting Opportunities".

All above from Z' to Z' plus 32 in Sectors I & II and Z' to Z'plus 48 Sectors III and IV at which times 4.5"Hows to lift at once to line marked for arrival at Z' plus 84.

This 18-pdr Standing Barrage to remain until Creeper reaches line 60/64, when all 18-pdrs in the Standing Barrage would at once jump to line marked 64/68 and then proceed by lifts as shown.

(b) Ammunition Z' to Z' plus 32 60% AX direct, for 18-pdrs and subsequently all A.

Rate of fire, 2 rounds per gun per minute, 18-pdrs from Z' to Z' plus 92 and thereafter as tactical situation and ammunition would allow, probably one round per gun per 4 minutes.

4.5" Hows. one round per How. per minute Z' to Z' plus 92 and then as above.

5. CREEPING BARRAGE.

(a) The creeping barrage would be formed as follows, <u>from batteries not moving.</u>

<u>Battle Wood Group.</u>   2 18-pdrs Sector I omitting that portion which lies south of a line drawn through J.31.d.55.15 to P.2.b.35.65.

<u>Canal Group.</u>   6 18-pdrs Sector II and inclusive of Southern portion of Sector I not covered by Battle Wood Group.

<u>Chateau Group.</u>   5 18-pdrs Sector III and an overlap in Sector IV of 250 yards all the way down the **dividing line** of the Sector.

<u>Oosthoek Group.</u>   2 18-pdrs Sector IV, less 250 yards Northern strip.

(b) Ammunition 3 rounds per gun per minute all A, Z' to Z' plus. On arriving at line 60/64, remains 4 minutes and at Z' plus 64 lifts direct to Limit or whatever line is ordered using all AX.

At Z' plus 92 as tactical situation requires minimum 1 round per gun per 4 minutes.

(c) To carry out above Chateau Group would be responsible for a strip 250 yards wide South of the dividing line Sectors III and IV both in Creeping and Standing Barrages.

Lieut, R.F.A.
Adjutant St.Eloi Artillery Group.

July 30th, 1917.

H4580

From:- Adjutant St Eloi Artillery Group.
To:- Officers Commanding Batteries.

Reference Creeping Barrage Table - AMMUNITION :-

"For 75% AX Direct" read "50% AX Direct".

Lieut.R.F.A.
Adjutant St Eloi Artillery Group.

July 30th.1917.

From:- Adjutant St Eloi Artillery Group.   H4579

To:- Officer Commanding C/104th. Brigade R.F.A.

AMENDMENT TO STANDING BARRAGE TABLE.

"After arriving there at Z plus 46" insert "at Z plus 50 lift to a line O.12.b.80.55. to O.12.d.95.15.".

This line will be marked "E" on Standing Barrage Map.

Lieut. R.F.A.
Adjutant St Eloi Artillery Group.

July 30th. 1917.

CREEPING BARRAGE.

TABLE.

TIME.	C/187.	B/187.	A/187.
Z to Z plus 4.	O.11.a.90.65.- O.11.a.85.45.	O.11.a.85.45.- O.11.a.80.25.	O.11.a.80.25.- O.11.a.75.10.
Z plus 4 to Z plus 8.	O.11.b.20.65.- O.11.b.12.45.	O.11.b.12.45.- O.11.b.00.25.	O.11.b.00.25.- O.11.a.95.05.
Z plus 8 to Z plus 10.	O.11.b.50.65.- O.11.b.37.45.	O.11.b.37.45.- O.11.b.25.25.	O.11.b.25.25.- O.11.b.10.05.
Z plus 10 to Z plus 14.	O.11.b.80.65.- O.11.b.67.45.	O.11.b.67.45.- O.11.b.50.25.	O.11.b.50.25.- O.11.b.30.00.
Z plus 14 to Z plus 22.	O.12.a.05.60.- O.11.b.92.45.	O.11.b.92.45.- O.11.b.72.20.	O.11.b.72.20.- O.11.d.50.95.
Z plus 22 to Z plus 26.	O.12.a.30.60.- O.12.a.12.42.	O.12.a.12.42.- O.11.b.95.25.	O.11.b.95.25.- O.11.d.70.95.
Z plus 26 to Z plus 40.	O.12.a.45.60.- O.12.a.25.42.	O.12.a.25.42.- O.12.a.00.22.	Pivots on right flank to O.12.a.00.22.
Z plus 40 to Z plus 44.	O.12.a.65.60.- O.12.a.45.40.	O.12.a.45.40.- O.12.a.20.20.	O.12.a.20.20.- O.11.d.95.95.
Z plus 44 to Z plus 48.	O.12.a.85.60.- O.12.a.65.42.	O.12.a.65.42.- O.12.a.40.17.	O.12.a.40.17.- O.12.c.15.95.
Z plus 48 to Z plus 52.	O.12.b.05.60.- O.12.a.85.40.	O.12.a.85.40.- O.12.a.62.17.	O.12.a.62.17.- O.12.c.40.95.
Z plus 52 to Z plus 56.	O.12.b.25.60.- O.12.b.05.40.	O.12.b.05.40.- O.12.a.82.15.	O.12.a.82.15.- O.12.c.60.95.
Z plus 56 to "Stop".	O.12.b.45.60.- O.12.b.25.37.	O.12.b.25.37.- O.12.b.00.12.	O.12.b.00.12.- O.12.c.85.95.

AMMUNITION.- All "A" from Z to Z plus 115, after Z plus 115 75% "AX" Direct

On completion of programme, 50% of guns in creeping barrage batteries will search and sweep 500 yards in advance of protective barrage line, i.e. last line of barrage using 75% "AX" Direct.

Rates of fire.
Z to Z plus 4............ 4 rounds per gun per minute.
Z plus 4 to Z plus 40.... 3 "   "   "   "   "
Z plus 40 to Z plus 99... 2 "   "   "   "   "
Z plus 99 to Z plus 115.. 3 "   "   "   "   "
Z plus 115 to Z plus 150. 1 "   "   "   "   "

Lieut. R.F.A.
Adjutant St Eloi Artillery Group.

July 23rd.1917.

H4578

From:- Adjutant St Eloi Artillery Group.

To:- Officers Commanding Batteries.

AMENDMENT TO CREEPING BARRAGE TABLE.

Last line and after to read :-

At Zero plus 56 to Zero plus 103 :-

C/187 - O.12.b.45.60. to O.12.b.95.37.
B/187 - O.12.b.95.37. to O.12.b.00.12.
A/187 - O.12.b.00.12. to O.12.c.85.95.

At Zero plus 103 to "Stop" :-

C/187 - O.12.b.68.60. to O.12.b.35.35.
B/187 - O.12.b.35.35. to O.12.b.05.10.
A/187 - Pivots on right flank to O.12.b.05.10.

Lieut.R.F.A.
Adjutant St Eloi Artillery Group.

July 30th.1917.

N4518

From:- Adjutant St Eloi Artillery Group.

To:- Officers Commanding Batteries.

AMENDMENT TO STANDING AND CREEPING BARRAGE.

Standing Barrage. line 2, substitute the following,
"At Zero plus 6 will search back from line AA to line C in three lifts, arriving on line C on the third lift at plus 12. First lift must be a clear 150 yards. Each lift to be of two minutes duration".
Map D in consequence of above, times on line C should read "plus 12 to plus 30".

Standing and Creeping Barrage.
    Zero to Zero plus 4...............4 rounds per gun per minute.
    Zero plus 4 to Zero plus 18...3   "   "   "   "   "
    Zero plus 18 to Zero plus 22..4   "   "   "   "   "
    Zero plus 22 to Zero plus 36..2   "   "   "   "   "
    Zero plus 36 to Zero plus 40..4   "   "   "   "   "
    Zero plus 40 to Zero plus 99..2   "   "   "   "   "
    Zero plus 99 to Zero plus 115.1   "   "   "   "   "
From Zero plus 115 at a minimum rate of 1 round per gun per 4 minutes until "Stop" is ordered.

Lieut.R.F.A.
Adjutant St Eloi Artillery Group.

July 28th.1917.

4.5"HOWITZER STANDING BARRAGE.

Reference - attached map.

Z to Z plus 6, 1 gun on FORRET FARM, remainder on "Brown Line" in Group Zone marked "AA"
Z plus 6 to Z plus 50, on "Red Line" in Group Zone marked "BB"
At Z plus 50, advance by lifts of 200 yards every 4 minutes to line in Group Zone marked "CC" and remain on this line till stop.

Rate of fire.
Z to Z plus 10......... 2 rounds per how per minute.
Z plus 10 to Z plus 60. 1   "   "   "   "   "
Z plus 60 to Z plus 90. 1   "   "   "   "   two minutes.
Z plus 90 to "Stop".... 1   "   "   "   "   four   "

Jon C Hunter
Lieut.R.F.A.
Adjutant St Eloi Artillery Group.

July 23rd.1917.

18-pdr. STANDING BARRAGE.

At Zero 18-pdr standing barrage opens on line in Group Zone marked AA.
At Zero plus 8 jumps direct from line AA to line in Group Zone marked C.
At Zero plus 30 it searches back in 4 lifts resting 4 minutes after each lift to line in Group Zone marked D, arriving there at Zero plus 46.
At Zero plus 60 it searches and sweeps 500 yards in Group Zone East of line D in various lifts till "Stop".

Rates of fire. Z to Z plus 4............ 4 rounds per gun per minute.
Z plus 4 to Z plus 40... 3   "   "   "   "   "
Z plus 40 to Z plus 99.. 2   "   "   "   "   "
Z plus 99 to Z plus 115. 3   "   "   "   "   "
Z plus 115 to Z plus 150 1   "   "   "   "   "
At Z plus 150 minimum rate of 1 round per gun per 4 minutes in bursts till "stop" if ordered.

Ammunition.   Z to Z plus 30............ 50% "AX" with Delay.
Z plus 30 to Z plus 46.. All "A".
Z plus 46 to "Stop"...... 75% "AX" Direct.

Lieut. R.F.A.
Adjutant St Eloi Artillery Group.

July 23rd, 1917.

From:- Adjutant St Eloi Artillery Group.

To:- Officers Commanding Batteries.

ADDENDUM TO BARRAGE TABLES.

18-pdr Standing Barrage, Rates of fire, last line, for "till stop if ordered" read "till stop is Ordered".

18-pdr Creeping Barrage, Rates of fire, add the following :- At Z plus 150 minutes rate of 1 round per gun per 4 minutes in bursts till "stop" is ordered.

18-pdr Creeping Barrage, At Z plus 20 creeping barrage batteries will fire 2 rounds smoke shell per 18-pdr Battery.

Lieut. R.F.A.
Adjutant St Eloi Artillery Group.

July 24th. 1917.

SECRET.   COPY No. 9

41st. DIVISIONAL ARTILLERY INSTRUCTION No. 8.

THE ADVANCE.   20-7-17.

Reference Maps Special HOLLEBEKE 'G' and Map attached.
Special 8150/1

1. Should opportunity offer it may be necessary to exploit a success by an attack on the ZANDVOORDE Line.
   To support such an attack it will be necessary to move Artillery forward.

2. GENERAL ARRANGEMENTS.

   NORTH GROUP. (a) One new forward Group will be formed North of the CANAL under orders of present O.C. BLUFF Group consisting of A/235, C/235, D/235, D/47, approximate positions shown in Map 'G' attached
   Remaining 18 pdr. batteries to be placed - B/235 and C/47 under command of O.C. CANAL Group - A/236 under command of O.C. CHATEAU Group

   BATTLE WOOD GROUP. (b) Will move forward A/104, B/104, C/189 to positions in I.34.c. to remain under orders O.C. BATTLE WOOD Group.

   CANAL GROUP. (c) No change except that B/235 and C/47 are added from BLUFF Group.

   CHATEAU GROUP. (d) No change except that A/236 is added from BLUFF Group.

   OOSTHOEK GROUP. (e) Will move forward, B/190, C/190, D/190, C/11 Aus: to positions in O.4.a.& C. and O.3.d.

   ST.ELOI GROUP. (f) Whole Group will advance to positions shown (approx:) in O.9.b.

3. **ROUTES.** Routes to be used for the advance are marked by boards, and lettered as under :-
   - For NORTH Group .. .. Route A.
   - "   BATTLE WOOD Group .. .. .. "   B.
   - "   OOSTHOEK Group .. .. .. "   C.
   - "   ST.ELOI Group .. .. .. "   D.

   Group Commanders are responsible that officers and senior N.C.O's are made personally acquainted with these Routes.

   ORDER to move. The actual order to move forward will be issued by this office to Groups.

4. The rotation in which Groups will advance must depend largely on the tactical situation.
   On receipt of orders to move Group Commanders should move forward first those Batteries which are most out-ranged.

5. **AMMUNITION.** As it is probable that the supply of ammunition will have to be by pack transport, ammunition carriers have been issued to Batteries, and a reserve of Carriers is held at the A.R.P. (N.4.c.5.4) for issue as required.

6. **REPORT.** Immediate report must be made to this office when any Battery arrives in action in it's new position - stating number of Battery and actual Map co-ordinate of position occupied.

7. **COMMUNICATIONS.** The buried lines available for use after advance are being communicated direct to Groups concerned. All other communications must be arranged by Groups.

41st. DIVISIONAL ARTILLERY INSTRUCTION No. 5 (Contd)

ZONES.
8. GROUP ZONES AFTER THE ADVANCE.

(a) O.C. NORTH Group will arrange to cover the whole Zone Front now covered by the three Northern Groups.

(b) The present BLUFF ZONE will be divided between BATTLE WOOD and CANAL GROUP - The boundary between these two Groups being an EAST and WEST line through road junction P.2.a.8.9 (inclusive to CHATEAU Group.)

(c) O.C. OOSTHOEK Group will arrange to cover the whole zone now covered by the three SOUTHERN Groups.

(d) The present OOSTHOEK Zone will be divided between CHATEAU and ST.ELOI Groups. Dividing line being an EAST and WEST line through road crossing P.8.a.3.9 (inclusive to CHATEAU Group).

Hugh Waller
Brigade Major,
41st. Divisional Artillery.

ISSUED at _____

Issued to all recipients of 41st. Divisional Artillery Order No.1
with addition of :-
C. R. E.
O.C. 41 Divnl. Signals.
41st. D.A. Signal Officer.

SECRET   COPY NO. 9

MEMORANDUM

25-7-17

In continuation of 41st D.A. Instruction No. 8.

1. The O.C., Bluff and St Eloi Groups should immediately reconnoitre for positions of assembly for their teams and vehicles in I.31.b and N.6.c., respectively. A report and rough tracing shewing suggested locations should be submitted as soon as possible.

2. In view of the absolute necessity of avoiding congestion on the routes of advance, it has been decided that the firing battery's only will move forward. The 1st Line Wagons remaining in their present wagon lines until ordered to move up to the position of assembly.
See para 6 below.
Firing Battery teams with vehicles full will be formed up at the assembly position at an hour to be notified later.

3. In each Group, limbers and firing battery wagons will be arranged so as to move forward in the following order:-

  (a) <u>Bluff Group</u>   A/235, C/235, D/235, B/235, D/47.

  (b) <u>St Eloi Group</u> C/104, C/187, B/187, A/187, D/187.

The first three Batteries in each Group will advance at the same time.
The last two, when the first three are reported in action.

Os.C. Groups concerned will arrange direct communication by any suitable means with their assembly positions. They must ensure that the sequence of Batteries, routes, etc., are thoroughly understood by all concerned.

Issue of Orders.
4. Orders for the commencement of the advance will be sent to Groups by this Office.
Groups will report as each battery gets into action.

The Advance.
5. Firing Battery wagons should proceed straight to the forward positions and dump their ammunition (unless specially ordered by the Group Commander to accompany its limber).
Guns will follow as soon as ready.

First line wagons.
6. First line wagons full should be kept ready harnessed up in their present wagon lines. Orders will be sent to them direct from this office, to move up to the assembly positions at the same time as orders are sent to Groups to advance their guns.
On arrival at the Assembly Positions first line wagons will come under orders of Group Commanders.

7. It is not intended to move Battle Wood and Oosthoek Groups until night of Z/A or morning of A day.

H W Waller.
Brigade Major
41st Divisional Artillery.

Issued at:-
Issued to all recipients of Instructions.
In addition 41st Div. Sigs., 41st D.A. Signs, C.R.E.

Map "G"

Route A

-33-

Good Route B

Route C Pontoon

Oosthoek
B/190
C/190
D/190
C/11 Aus.

-3-

Route D

St Eloi
A/187
B/187
C/187
D/187
C/104

-9- Legend

= 18 Pdrs Positions (approx)
△ = 4·5 How
= Tracks (approx)

Track A = Present Caterpillar Track
" B = Along N Bank Canal
" C = Oak Dump Road
" D = Pheasant Dump Road

184th Bde R.F.A.

WAR DIARY or INTELLIGENCE SUMMARY
Army Form C. 2118

August 1917.

Place	Date	Hour	Summary of Events and Information	Remarks and references to Appendices
August 1st 1917		—	Brigade reorganised by 6/104 in action as from July 20th (HdQrs "Deal Dog Farm")	
	2nd	6.0 a.m.	6/104 fired 55 rounds on O.12.b.	
		10.0 a.m. to 2.30 p.m.	50 rounds BX on Machine Guns in O.12.b. A/189 20 rounds on Transport.	
			Night firing:— 250 rds A+AX on P.Y.a.10.25 – P.7.a.80.40, P.Y.a.05.20 – P.Y.c.65.65. 95 rds BX " "	
	3rd		Hostile Artillery active in forward area — Casualties — 1 wounded.	
			Night firing:— 250 rds A+AX on rounds as on August 2nd. 95 rds BX " "	
	4th	12 Noon to 6.0 p.m.	100 rds AX on P.8.t. 05.y.0.	
		12 Noon to 2.5 p.m.	100 rds AX on Hollebeke Nise + 50 rds BX on Hollebeke Nise	
		3.25 p.m.	38 rds on Lock 5.	
			Hostile Artillery active in forward area — Casualties 3 OR wounded.	
			Night firing:— 250 rds A+AX on rds as on August 2nd. 95 rds BX " " "	
			1 Section of 6/104 relieved by 1 Section of 124th Battery	
	5th	5.0 a.m.	S.O.S. — Barrage in Hollebeke	
		6.0 a.m.	Barrage 40/44 Guns	
		9.50 a.m.	Laytam 100 y rds.	
		10.45 a.m.	Barrage reported clear of Hollebeke	9.0–10.15a.m. 50 yrds AX on O.12.a.2.0. – O.11.d.95.95. 80 rds BX " Lock 5.

WAR DIARY or INTELLIGENCE SUMMARY

Army Form C. 2118

(Erase heading not required.)

Place	Date	Hour	Summary of Events and Information	Remarks and references to Appendices
August 5th	1917	2.15 p.m.	S.O.S. Lines, 208 rds A + AX, 80 rds B.X.	
		9.30 p.m.	S.O.S.	
		10.45 p.m.	Orders received to stop firing.	
	6th	2.0 a.m. to 2.10 a.m.	380 rds AX + 30 rds BX fired on S.O.S. Barrage lines, searching East by lifts of 100 yards, resting two minutes on each lift.	
		3.0 a.m. to 3.20 a.m.	380 rds AX + 30 rds BX fired on S.O.S. Barrage lines as above.	
		4.5 a.m. to 4.25 a.m.	560 rds AX + 60 rds BX fired on S.O.S. Barrage lines as above.	
		9.0 a.m.	40 rds BX on C and B and at 0.12.b.3.5. — 0.12.b.4.0.	
		9.36 a.m.	390 rds A + AX on 200 yards beyond S.O.S. with lifts of 100 yards, back to 500 yards beyond S.O.S. Hostile Artillery active in front areas to own batteries, D/187 shelled during afternoon — 1 gun knocked out, 3 OR wounded.	
			New S.O.S. lines :— 124 of B battery 0.12.b.0.6. — 0.12.a.80.45.	
			C/189 0.12.a.80.45. — 0.12.a.58.25.	
			B/187 0.12.a.58.25. — 0.12.a.38.19.	
			A/187 0.12.a.38.19. — 0.12.c.15.95.	
			D/187 2 hours on Lock 5 remainder superimposed on own from 0.12.b.0.6. — 0.12.c.15.95.	
			Night firing :— 350 rds A + AX on roads P.7.a. & P.7.c. 95 rds BX " "	

WAR DIARY
or
INTELLIGENCE SUMMARY
(Erase heading not required.)

Army Form C. 2118

Place	Date	Hour	Summary of Events and Information	Remarks and references to Appendices
August	7th 1917	2.40 a.m. to 2.55 a.m.	B/187 Bombards Canal Railway Embankment from 0.12.b.8.0. - 0.12.b.50.39. (1 rd per gun per minute)	
		4.8 a.m. to 4.23 a.m.		
		2.55 a.m. 3.0 a.m. 4.23 a.m. to 4.28 a.m.	A, B & C/187 Barrage fire as follows at 2 rounds per gun per minute :— 50% AX. A/187 0.12.d. 80.90. - 0.12.b. 50.03 B/187 0.12.b. 50.03. - 0.12.b. 45.15. C/187 0.12.b. 45.15. - 0.12.b. 35.95.	
		3.5 a.m. & 3.10 a.m. 4.33 a.m. to 4.38 a.m.	A, B & C/187 Barrage fire as follows at 2 rounds per gun per minute :— 50% AX. A/187 0.12.c. 30.95. - 0.12.c. 45.65. B/187 0.12.c. 45.65. - 0.12.c. 65.95. C/187 0.12.c. 65.95. - 0.12.c. 80.00.	
		4.30 pm	20 rds BX on suspected machine gun 0.12.a. 38.10. - 0.12.c. 15.95.	
			A/187 heavily shelled — 4 OR's wounded.	
		3.0 pm	Night firing :— 250 rds A + AX on rds P.y.a. & P.y.c. 95 rds BX	
8th	—	3.30 pm to 6.0 pm	45 rounds on registration.	
			S.O.S. lines re-distributed between C & A/187, 124th Battery, 117th Battery having relieved 119th Battery at 0.3.c. 62.42.	
			Night firing :— 250 rds A + AX on roads P.y.c. & P.y.c. 250 rds BX	
9th	—	6.45 pm 9.10 pm	Group Shoots at 3 times during the day on P.y.c. 80. 98. KASTELHOEK. S.O.S. G. Star Down. Gun Night Firing :— 250 rds A & AX 95 rds BX on roads P.y.a. & P.y.c.	

Army Form C. 2118.

WAR DIARY
or
INTELLIGENCE SUMMARY
(Erase heading not required.)

Instructions regarding War Diaries and Intelligence Summaries are contained in F. S. Regs., Part II. and the Staff Manual respectively. Title Pages will be prepared in manuscript.

Place	Date	Hour	Summary of Events and Information	Remarks and references to Appendices
	August 10th 1917	—	Hostile Artillery very active in forward area, Enemy area received some attention in afternoon.	
		8.55pm to 9.22pm	Gas Shell bombardment by D/187 on O.12.d. 85.95. Night firing:- 250 rds A 7A X on road P.7.a. & P.7.c.	
	11th	12.5pm 2.34pm 5.30pm	} Concentrated Shoots by A, B, C/187	
		5.0 a.m. 6.55pm to 9.22pm	Gas Shell Bombardment by D/187 on O.12.d. 85.95. Gas Shell Bombardment by D/187 on O.12.d. 85.95.	
			Night firing:- 250 rds A 7A X on road P.7.a. & P.7.c. Gas Shell Bombardment by D/187 on O.12.d. 85.95.	
	12th	5.0am 3.15pm 5.45pm 6.20pm	} Concentrated Shoots by A, B, C/187.	
			Night firing:- 250 rds A 7A X on road P.7.a. & P.7.c. 95 - BX	
	13th	6.0am 2.10pm 4.5pm 7.25pm	} Concentrated Shoots by A. B. C. D/187. Damage found on tanks, Difch Army Tanks.	
			Hostile artillery active near batteries.	
	Night 13/14		Night firing:- 250 rds A 7A X & 95 Bx on road P.7.a. & P.7.c. Relieved by 116th Bde (3 gas 70 incens)	

1875 Wt.W593/826 1,000,000 4/15 J.B.C. & A. A.D.S.S./Forms/C. 2118.

Army Form C. 2118

WAR DIARY
or
INTELLIGENCE SUMMARY
(Erase heading not required.)

Instructions regarding War Diaries and Intelligence Summaries are contained in F. S. Regs., Part II. and the Staff Manual respectively. Title Pages will be prepared in manuscript.

Place	Date	Hour	Summary of Events and Information	Remarks and references to Appendices
	August 14th 1917	12.50 pm / 3.30 pm / 8.30 pm	} Concentrate Shoots by A, B, C rds/187.	
	Night 14/15th	Night	Night firing :- 250 rds on road P.7.a. r.P.7.c. 95 rds BX 124 & Jap B de recvn by 114/k Jap B de (3 got 20 missing)	
	15th	1.0 pm / 4.30 pm / 7.0 pm	} Concentrate Shoots by A, B, C rds/187.	
			Hostile Artillery active in forward area, 6 casualties – 2 OR's wounded.	
	16th	12 noon / 2.0 pm / 2.05 pm	} Night firing :- 250 rds on road P.7.a. + P.7.c. 95 rds BX " " " " Concentrate Shoots by A, B, C rds/187.	
	17th	1.30 pm / 4.0 pm / 8.15 pm	} Night firing :- 250 rds on road P.7.a. r.P.7.c. 95 rds BX " " " " Concentrate Shoots by A, B, C rds/187.	
	18th	2.0 pm / 4.45 pm / 6.30 pm	} Concentrate Shoots by A, B rds/187. Night firing :- 250 rds ATPTX on road P.7.a. r.P.7.c. 95 rds BX " " " "	

Army Form C. 2118

WAR DIARY
or
INTELLIGENCE SUMMARY

(Erase heading not required.)

Instructions regarding War Diaries and Intelligence Summaries are contained in F. S. Regs., Part II. and the Staff Manual respectively. Title Pages will be prepared in manuscript.

Place	Date	Hour	Summary of Events and Information	Remarks and references to Appendices
August 19th		2.30pm 3.45pm 7.15pm	} Concentrated Shoots by A, B, C vd)117.	
			Hostile Artillery active in forward areas.	
			Night firing:— 250 rds A.PX on roads P.7.a. P.7.c. 95 rds BX	
	20th	8.0 am 11.30 am 4.30 pm	} Concentrated Shoots by A, B, C vd)187.	
			Night firing:— 250 rds A.PX on roads P.7.a. P.7.c., + wire at P.7.b. 6.5 & P.7.b. 6.4.y.	
	21st	1.30 pm 4.0 pm 7.45 pm	} Concentrated Shoots by A, B, C vd)187.	
			Night firing:— 150 rds A.PX on roads P.7.a. P.7.c.	
	22nd	4.0 am	Barrage fired in co-operation with attack by 2nd inf.	
		1.30 pm 2.15 pm 3.30 pm	} Concentrated Shoots by A, B, C vd)187.	
			Hostile Artillery active in forward areas.	
			Night firing:— 150 rds A.PX on roads P.7.a. P.7.c.	
	23rd	8.0 am 11.0 am 2.30 pm	} Concentrated Shoots Districts hit by A.P.C & vd)187.	
			Night firing:— 150 rds A.PX on roads P.7.a. P.7.c. 116th Infy B. de relieved by 119th Infy B. de (39th Division)	

Army Form C. 2118.

WAR DIARY
or
INTELLIGENCE SUMMARY
(Erase heading not required.)

Instructions regarding War Diaries and Intelligence Summaries are contained in F. S. Regs., Part II. and the Staff Manual respectively. Title Pages will be prepared in manuscript.

Place	Date	Hour	Summary of Events and Information	Remarks and references to Appendices
August 24th	1919	12 Noon	Took over responsibility for Gostrch Group front in addition to own. Received by A 78/119 B & R 2a. Southern Boundary — a line through 6.11 central M 29.c.00.85. Northern Boundary — a line through O.c.c.00.90 + P.1.d.00.85. New S.O.S. line as follows:— A/187) O.12.c.40.95. — O.12.a.65.25. B/187) O.12.a.65.25. — O.12.b.00.60. — O.12.b.02.70. A/119) O.12.b.02.70. — O.c.d.20.30. B/119) O.c.d.20.30. — O.c.d.40.88. C/187) Superimposed on where first. A/187) 1 Stow each on:— Rock 5, and quarry at O.12.c.50.30. b and c wiring at 8.12.b.68.02. Junction of Red Road Rock 5 to O.12.d.95.95. Cemetery b and c from Rock 5 to O.12.b.15.85. Junction of Tracks at O.c.d.80.40. C/187 not to fire on S.O.S. except on orders from this Office.	
		12.30pm 2.30pm 4.15pm	} Concentrated shots on Eleck Farm by A, B, C & D/187. A 78/119. Night firing :— 200 rds A.P.K. on roads M 29.a. M 29.c. & Eleck Farm.	
	25th	2.30pm 5.0pm 6.0pm	} Concentrated shots by Batteries. Hostile Artillery active in forward area. Back Area searched with gas shell during night. Night firing :— 200 rds A.P.K. on roads P.7.a., P.7.c. & O.G.d. Gasts dropped on track near by hostile planes during night.	

2449. Wt. W14957/Mg0 750,000 1/16 J.B.C. & A. Forms/C.2118/12.

WAR DIARY
or
INTELLIGENCE SUMMARY

(Erase heading not required.)

Army Form C. 2118.

Instructions regarding War Diaries and Intelligence Summaries are contained in F. S. Regs., Part II. and the Staff Manual respectively. Title Pages will be prepared in manuscript.

Place	Date	Hour	Summary of Events and Information	Remarks and references to Appendices
August 26th 1917		5.0 pm / 6.15 pm / 7.35 pm	Concentrated Shoots by Batteries	
	27th	2.30 am	Night Shoot :— 200 rds A.P.S.R. on roads P.7.a., P.7.c. & O.6.d.	
			Evening fire no co-operation with raid carried out by Division on our right on BEE FARM at O.23.b.10.55.	
		2.0 pm	Concentrated Shoot by Batteries.	
	28th		Night Shoot :— 200 rds A.P.S.R. on roads P.7.a., P.7.c & O.6.d. Bombs dropped on Bock Area by hostile planes during night.	
		12 Noon	Concentrated Shoot on O.6.d. 50.00. by Batteries	
			Hostile Artillery very quiet.	
	29th		Night Shoot :— 200 rds A.P.S.R. on roads P.7.a., P.7.c. & O.6.d.	
		3.0 pm	Concentrated Shoot on P.1.d. 25.00. — P.7.b. 25.00. by Batteries	
			Night Shoot :— 300 rds A.P.S.R. on roads P.7.a., P.7.c & O.6.d. 60 rds Bx " " "	
	30th	7.30 am	Concentrated Shoot on P.1.d. 25.00. — P.7.b. 25.00. by Batteries	
			Night Shoot :— 300 rds A.P.S.R. on roads P.7.a., P.7.c. & O.6.d. 60 rds Bx " " "	

Army Form C. 2118.

WAR DIARY
or
INTELLIGENCE SUMMARY

(Erase heading not required.)

Instructions regarding War Diaries and Intelligence Summaries are contained in F. S. Regs., Part II. and the Staff Manual respectively. Title Pages will be prepared in manuscript.

Place	Date	Hour	Summary of Events and Information	Remarks and references to Appendices
August 31st	1917	—	Command of Br. Eni. Group (184 Bde B. A.) passed from Lt. Col. J. Symonds, D.S.O., R.F.A. to Lt. Col. J. Summers, R.F.A. 104th Army Brigade R.F.A. at 11.0 a.m.	
	Sep 3/1/17		A R/184 AT Brig R.F.A. withdrawn to repair tires. One section of B R/184 AT Brig R.F.A. relieved by one section of C R/104th Italy 184 AT Brig R.F.A. moved into Reserve BOESCHEPE area.	

J. Summers
Lieut. Colonel, R.F.A.
Commanding 104th Brigade R.F.A.

2449 Wt. W14957/M90 750,000 1/16 J.B.C. & A. Forms/C.2118/12.

184th Brigade R.F.A.

WAR DIARY
or
INTELLIGENCE SUMMARY

September 1917

Army Form C. 2118.

Vol 17

Instructions regarding War Diaries and Intelligence Summaries are contained in F. S. Regs., Part II. and the Staff Manual respectively. Title Pages will be prepared in manuscript.

(Erase heading not required.)

Place	Date	Hour	Summary of Events and Information	Remarks and references to Appendices
September 1917				
	Night 1/2nd	—	Kept return in BOESCHEPE area, since August 31st.	
	2nd-12 Noon	—	Remaining two sections of B/184 returned by two Sections of C/184 & D/184 dubs. J. A.	
	3rd - 6th	—	Batteries remain in BOESCHEPE area, also D/190 Bde R.F.A. (under us for administrative purposes)	
	7th	—	Nothing of importance to report.	
		—	Each Battery now consists 1 Officer & 12 men known as forward parties as under: —	
			A/184 H. 28. b. 45. 45.	
			B/184 H. 28. a. 85. 55.	
			C/184 H. 29. a. 60. 30. } Sheet 28 S.W.	
			D/184 H. 28. b. 80. 35.	
			D/190 H. 28. d. 20. 80.	
	8th - 10th	—	Nothing of importance to report.	
	11th 5.0 pm	—	Received orders for batteries to move to Wagon Lines in N.3.b. & N.4.a.	
	12th 10.0 am	—	A/184 left Boeschepe for Wagon Lines in N.3.b. & N.4.a.	
	10.30 am	—	B/184 "	
	11.0 am	—	C/184 "	
	11.30 am	—	D/184 "	
	12 Noon	—	D/190 "	
	12 Noon	—	D/190 passes under control of its own Bde. etc.	

Army Form C. 2118.

WAR DIARY
or
INTELLIGENCE SUMMARY

(Erase heading not required.)

Instructions regarding War Diaries and Intelligence Summaries are contained in F. S. Regs., Part II. and the Staff Manual respectively. Title Pages will be prepared in manuscript.

Place	Date	Hour	Summary of Events and Information	Remarks and references to Appendices
September	12/13th/1917	—	One Section of A, B D/189 occupied position prepared by storm. One Section of C/189 relieved one Section of A/186 B/S R2a at I.28.a.65.15.	
	13th	12 Noon	Staff moved from Boesinghe to Morgan Rein in N.3.b. & N.4.a.	
	Night 13/14th	—	Remaining Section of A, B, & D/189 occupy positions as above.	
	14th 4.0 pm	—	Staff move from Morgan Rein to hut rock 8, & reoccupy by D/189 Bde R2a, Brigade is known as "Symonds Group", & comes under tactical control of 39th Divisional Artillery. S.O.S. Zone of Group:— From J.20.c.12.42½ – J.26.a.08.80. D/94 (Bde R2a) at I.22.d.23.12, leaves to 234th Divisional Artillery for "Night Firing" tasks. Night firing by B/189:— 150 rds AX on Road from J.20.d.60.00 – J.20.d.80.00. " " C/189:— 150 rds AX on J.20.c.97.27.	
	15th	11.0 pm	Gas Shell bombardment by D/189 on target given by "Symonds Group". Preparatory (D) barrage commenced.	
		8.0.0.8	6 of Barrage No 4 fired by A. B. & C/189 & D/94.	
		4.0 pm	Cont Barrage No 3 fired by A. B. & D/189 & D/94.	
		1.0 "	Hostile Artillery very active in Boesinghe Area — 1 Officer + 1 O.R. wounded.	
		6.0 "		
		2.0 pm	Night firing:— 275 rds A9AX + 245 rds BX on road at J.24.a.95.19. 365 rds A9AX on J.20.d.00.05. 282 rds A+AX on Wire from J.20.c.90.05 – J.20.c.95.30.	

WAR DIARY or INTELLIGENCE SUMMARY

Army Form C. 2118.

(Erase heading not required.)

Place	Date	Hour	Summary of Events and Information	Remarks and references to Appendices
September	16th 1917	10.0 am	Barrage on Army front by B. Battery.	
		11.0 am	95 rds A.P.X on Wire from J.20.c.80.00. – J.20.c.95.30.	
			90 rds B.X on J.20.c.65.15. – J.20.c.10.00.	
		12 noon	Hostile Artillery generally active throughout the day – Casualties Nil.	
			Enemy activity by hostile aircraft over Divnl Area.	
		6.0 pm	Retal: Barrage No.2 fired by B. Battery.	
			Night firing:- Gas Shell bombardment on J.26.c.98.50. – J.27.a.30.82.	
			250 rds A.P.X on J.27.a. 95.19.	
			350 rds A.P.X on J.20.c. 90.24.	
			193 rds on Wire from J.20.c. 80.00. – J.20.c. 95.30.	
	17th	—	Hostile increased Infantry counterattack in Divnl Area.	
		5.0 am	Retal: Barrage No.2 reported by B. Battery.	
			90 rds B.X on J.20.c. 65.15. – J.20.c. 10.00.	
		9.0 am	95 rds A.T.P.X on Wire from J.20.c. 80.00. – J.20.c. 95.30.	
			Reported destruction shoots by hostile artillery on trench transport on the day.	
		3.0 pm	Retal Barrage No.1 fired by B. Battery.	
			225 rds A.P.X on Road J.20.d. 3.0. – J.26.b. 60.95.	
			22.5 rds B.X "	
			315 rds A.T.P.X on J.20.b. 00.05.	
			286 rds A.P.X on Wire from J.20.c. 80.00. – J.20.c. 95.30.	
			Night firing:- Infantry column reported of 234 & 3 gft 10 inninio	
	Night 17/18th	—	Hd M.O. received Army Front by Battery.	
	18th	6.0 am	Barrage on Army front by Battery.	
		7.0 am	S.O.S. Hd M.O. assumed command of Hd M.R. avenue Offensive Front.	

WAR DIARY or INTELLIGENCE SUMMARY

Army Form C. 2118.

(Erase heading not required.)

Place	Date	Hour	Summary of Events and Information	Remarks and references to Appendices
September 18th		7.0 am 1917	B.S.R.A. 41st MGC winning assumed responsibility for Artillery Defence of front. Regiment Group came under command of B.S.R.A. 41st Division.	
		8.0 am	95 R/R A.A.A. on Wire J.20.c.80.05. – J.20.c.95.30.	
		9.45 am	90 R/R B.X. on J.20.c.65.15. – J.20.c.10.00.	
			Hostile Artillery very active throughout the day. Casualties – 1 OR killed, 2 OR wounded.	
		6.30 pm	Barrage on Army front by batteries.	
			Night Firing:- 225 R/R A.X. on Road J.20.d.3.0. – J.26.b.60.95.
			225 R/R B.X. " " J.20.c.80.60. – J.20.c.95.30.
			315 R/R A.A.A. on J.20.d.00.05.
			280 R/R on Wire from J.20.c.80.60. – J.20.c.95.30.
	19th	10.0 am	90 R/R B.X. on J.20.c.65.15. – J.20.c.10.00.	
			95 R/R A.A.A. on Wire from J.20.c.80.60. – J.20.c.95.30.	
		3.0 pm	Batteries open fire. Artillery day fired by batteries. Hostile Artillery active in forward areas. Casualties – 3 OR wounded, 4 OR's gassed.	
			Night Firing:- 225 R/R A.X. on Road from J.20.d.3.0. – J.26.b.6.0.95.
			225 R/R B.X. " "
			315 R/R A.A.A. on J.20.c.97.27.
			10 R/R A.A.A. on Wire from J.20.c.80.00. – J.20.c.95.30.
	20th	5.40 am	Barrage fired in conjunction with attack by 41st Division infantry on "Beau" & "Gem" trenches from North of BODMIN COPSE to LOWER STAR POST. Hostile artillery very active during morning. Casualties – 1 Officer wounded, 1 OR killed, 15 OR's wounded & 1 OR gassed. 2 guns put out of action. S.O.S. – Artillery responded perfectly. Fire from Protector Row, Thompson's	
		7.34 pm		

WAR DIARY
or
INTELLIGENCE SUMMARY

(Erase heading not required.)

Army Form C. 2118.

Instructions regarding War Diaries and Intelligence Summaries are contained in F.S. Regs., Part II. and the Staff Manual respectively. Title Pages will be prepared in manuscript.

Place	Date	Hour	Summary of Events and Information	Remarks and references to Appendices
September 20th	1917	9.0 pm	D/94 H.B. reported to O.C. forces tremens of South Group. Our line runs along Zonne line in far south as J.21.c.6.4. — J.26.b.2.6. thence along W. BASSEVILLE BEEKE to J.26.a.4.9. — J.20.a.95.40. — J.20.d.9.6. Up to 6.30 pm 3 O[ther].R[ank]s and 96 O.R.s had arrived through Divisional Prisoners of War Cage, belonging to 4th Bav. R.I.R., R.I.R., 28th Ersatz, 39th I.R. 15th R.I.R.	
	21st	5.30 am	A/189 moved to advanced position at I.24.c.25.35.	
		6.0 am to 9.30 am	D/189 fired on position June at J.26.b.85.05, & at J.27.a.20.85 in co-operation with barrage for attack by 128th Inf.Bde on Stroy Point J.29.a.15.80. — J.26.a.80.90. — Shown batty were him	
		10.0 a.m.	Registrations by A/189.	
		2.0 pm	B/189 moved to advanced position at I.24.c.80.50.	
		3.0 pm to 3.3 pm	Barrage in Protective S.O.S. line.	
			Hostile Artillery very active on Roads & round B. Battery Position in vicinity of ZILLEBEKE	
		6.0 pm to 7.30 pm 5.30 pm 7.30 pm	Cnt. Barrage by battalion, cancelled by S.O.S. on front.	
			S.O.S.	
	22nd	8.30 am	A/189 fired in Enfilade Barrage. 50 rds BX on J.29.a.25.80.	
		1.15 pm	Hostile Artillery very active on whole front area. Casualties — 9 O.R.s wounded	
		6.0 pm	A/189 heavily shelled — 1 gun knocked out.	

WAR DIARY
or
INTELLIGENCE SUMMARY
(Erase heading not required.)

Army Form C. 2118.

Instructions regarding War Diaries and Intelligence Summaries are contained in F. S. Regs., Part II. and the Staff Manual respectively. Title Pages will be prepared in manuscript.

Place	Date	Hour	Summary of Events and Information	Remarks and references to Appendices
September 22nd	1917	Night	Reports that forms in the tactical control of divisional Artillery. A, B, C/187 reinforced our front from J. 21.6. 85.00. & houses at J. 21.6. 86.83. Houses of avenue at J.15.d. 95.15. D/187 reinforced our front from J.22.c. 45.96., along railway embankment to J.22.a. 95.10. & new edge of wood at J.16.c. 94.10. 118th Lap.B.de (39th Division) relieved 124th & 125th Lap.Bdes (39th Division) between 122nd Lap.B.de in left sector & 6/187 rear to divisional front.	
	23rd	5.30 am	Corps B.group fired by Division Command of Artillery.	
		7.0 am	41st Division relieved in ZEVECOTEN & re-opened in CAESTRE.	
		10-0 am	H.Q. R.A. 41st Division close at I.30.a.50.80.	
		6.0 pm	D/187 moved to advanced position at I.24.c.40.10. until convey. 23rd Division took over front from J.21.6.32. to J.15.6.0.9. Afterwards B.group reinforced 23rd D.A. Levy reinforced our front from J.21.b.8.5. to houses at J.21.6.86.63. & wood I. west of J.15.d. Batteries shelled throughout day. Casualties 1 O.R. killed, 14 O.R.s wounded. Night Enemy:- 20 ms AX on MENIN Road from J.22.c.80.00 - J.22.d.00.60.	
	24th		Fine early morning, hostile artillery on any action throughout day. Our gunners no reports to trade no rounding & tried barrage & counter – 12 O.R.s wounded. Night Enemy:- 300 ms SAX on MENIN Road from J 22.c.80.00 - J.22.d.00.60.	
	Night 24/25		33rd D.D.w Infantry relieved 23rd Divisional Infantry between J.21.6.45.15. & northern edge of POLYGON WOOD.	

WAR DIARY or INTELLIGENCE SUMMARY

Army Form C. 2118.

Place	Date	Hour	Summary of Events and Information	Remarks and references to Appendices
September	25th '17	3.20am	Counter attack by enemy on our slightly firmed line.	
		4.0 am	28th Divisional Artillery H.Q. relieved by 33rd Divisional Artillery H.Q.	
			From 4.0 am S.O.S. Zones for Signals Group as follows:—	
			A/167 J.21.f.85.00 – J.15.d.95.00.	
			B/167 J.15.d.95.00 – J.15.c.10.40 – J.15.f.95.00.	
			C/167 J.15.b.95.00 – J.15.b.95.60 – J.10.c.20.00.	
			D/167 Superimposed over whole front.	
		2.15pm	Enemy Barrage fire by batteries.	
			Hostile Artillery very active around battery position – 3 guns knocked out, casualties – 1 OR killed 4 gunners & 23 ORs wounded.	
	29th	5.50am	Barrage fired in co-operation with attack by 33rd Division.	
			Retaliation on our batteries very severe, continuing throughout night. Casualties 3 ORs killed, 13 ORs gassed & 26 ORs wounded.	
			Night firing:— 250 rds A.T.H.X. on areas 300 yards East of S.O.S. line & 50 rds B.X. on S.O.S. lines as follows:—	
			B/167 J.16.c.95.55 – J.16.c.80.95.	
			C/167 J.16.c.80.95 – J.16.a.65.40.	
			D/167 Same as [?] above.	
	Night 30/6/17		A/167 withdrawn to [?] this battery are one gun extra to B & C/167 to complete.	

WAR DIARY
or
INTELLIGENCE SUMMARY
(Erase heading not required.)

Army Form C. 2118.

Place	Date	Hour	Summary of Events and Information	Remarks and references to Appendices
September 27/9/17		5.0 am	Barrage on S.O.S. line by batteries. Hostile artillery much quieter throughout day.	
	Night 27/28th		H/W, D, A, 76/187 withdrawn to Wagon Lines.	
28th			Guns rest at Wagon Lines.	
29th		3-18 pdr guns & 5-4.5 hows to 315th Army Bde near R.A.	
30th		10.0 am	Shutdown. Brigade marched from Wagon Lines to area of SHAEXKEN near BERTHEN (Sheet 27) Started over 15-18 pdr guns at old wagon lines to 113th Army Bde near R.A.	

[signature]
Lieut Colonel R.A.
Commanding 160th Brigade R.A.

30/9/17

184th Brigade R.F.A.

WAR DIARY
or
INTELLIGENCE SUMMARY

(Erase heading not required.)

October 1914

Army Form C. 2118.

Place	Date	Hour	Summary of Events and Information	Remarks and references to Appendices
October	1st 1914		Brigade in rest at SHAEXKEN (near BERTHEN) Sheet 24.	
	2nd to 4th		Nothing of importance to report.	
	5th		D/164 Bty took over from D/113th Brigade R.F.A. 5 4.5" Howitzers.	
	6th		A."B" & "C"/164 Bty took over from 39th Divisional Artillery 3 - 18 pdr guns each.	
	7th	4.30 a.m.	Brigade marched from SHAEXKEN en route for EHYVELDE (Sheet Dunkerque 1A). Arrived at WORMHOUDT about 1.30 p.m. & rested there for remainder of day.	
	8th	6.0 a.m.	Brigade marched from WORMHOUDT & arrived at EHYVELDE at 2.0 p.m. Inspected the road by G.O.C. 41st Division. Brigade in rest at EHYVELDE.	
	9th			
	10th		3 Officers, 4 N.C.Os. & 6 Signallers were found to 211 B.R.F.A. to remain with battery. These respective battures were relieving Battures drawn guns from 190th Bde R.F.A. & complete establishment.	

Army Form C. 2118.

WAR DIARY
or
INTELLIGENCE SUMMARY
(Erase heading not required.)

Place	Date	Hour	Summary of Events and Information	Remarks and references to Appendices
October 11th	1917 Night 11/12th		One section per battery returned. One section of each battery of 211th Brigade R.F.A. in R.29.c. + R.29.a. (Sheet 11)	
"	12/13th		Remaining section completed above relief.	
"	13th 12 Noon		Lieut Colonel G. Symonds, D.S.O. R.F.A. took over command of "G" Group from O.C. 211th Brigade R.F.A. Group composed of 3-18 pdr Batteries "A", "B", "C" 76/184. D/187 under tactical cmd of "A" Group (158th Bde.R.F.A.) S.O.S. tasks as follows:—
			A/184 M.23.a. 26.44. — M.22.b. 90.40.	
			B/184 M.22.b. 90.40. — M.22.b. 39.40.	
			C/184 M.22.b. 90.40. — M.22.a. 85.40.	
		11 to 3.0 pm	Allied fired 101 rounds A.P.X. on registration	
		2.15pm	Hostile artillery active in R.24.b., R.30.a., R.30.c. + R.29.b.	
		6.5 pm	Casualties Nil	

WAR DIARY
or
INTELLIGENCE SUMMARY
(Erase heading not required.)

Army Form C. 2118.

Place	Date	Hour	Summary of Events and Information	Remarks and references to Appendices
October	20th 1917	5.45pm (6.6pm)	B/189 fired 12 rounds A on registration. D/189 fired 12 rounds BX on hostile trench mortar "AMY". Hostile Artillery below normal.	
	21st	11.0 am	A/189 fired 10 rounds A & 20 rounds AX retaliation on hostile trench mortar "AMY".	
		5.30 p	A 189/189 fired 30 rounds AX each on M.15.c. 80.00. Hostile Artillery very quiet.	
	22nd		D/189 fired 30 rounds. Gas shell on M.17.a. 70.70. Heavy Artillery action & irregular retaliation throughout day. Hostile Artillery normal.	
	23rd	2.10 p	A/189 fired 30 rounds AX retaliation on hostile trench mortar "AMY".	
		3.0 p	B/189 fired 5 rounds BX on movement at M.15.t. 55.40.	
		3.35 p	D/189 fired 20 rounds BX retaliation on hostile trench mortar "AMY". Hostile Artillery active throughout day.	

Army Form C. 2118.

WAR DIARY
or
INTELLIGENCE SUMMARY

(Erase heading not required.)

Instructions regarding War Diaries and Intelligence Summaries are contained in F. S. Regs., Part II. and the Staff Manual respectively. Title Pages will be prepared in manuscript.

Place	Date	Hour	Summary of Events and Information	Remarks and references to Appendices
	October 24th 1917		Our artillery wire & telephone dug. Hostile Artillery quiet. Lieut Colonel F. Symonds, D.S.O, R.J.O, proceeded on leave. Brig ah command taken over by Major H. R. Ruston, R.J.A. D/187.	
	25th	6pm	D/187 fires 10 rounds BX in answer to N.F. Bell — M.x.8. Hostile Artillery action throughout day. Following are S.O.S. Zones for D/187 our ack from today:— Sunken Road at N. 15. d. 89. 00. — M. 16. c. 02. 25. Cross Roads " M. 15. d. 95. 30. " " M. 15. d. 95. 75. " " M. 15. b. 50. 00. Trenches at M. 15. central. M. 15. a. 50. 20.	
	26th		Our artillery wire & telephone dug. Hostile Artillery below normal.	
	27th	6.0am	Orders received for relief of Brigade by 58th Bde R.J.A. 9th Divisional to prepare to move elsewhere by land at short notice.	

WAR DIARY
or
INTELLIGENCE SUMMARY

(Erase heading not required.)

Army Form C. 2118.

Place	Date	Hour	Summary of Events and Information	Remarks and references to Appendices
	October 27th 1917		Our artillery inactive all day.	
	28th 1917		Hostile artillery active on roads in forward areas.	
	Night 28/29th		Enemy's trenches shelled, 1 gun destroyed, trench on causeways. One section of each battery relieved by one section of each battery of 50th Bde R.F.A. 9th Divisional Artillery.	
	29th	4.0 p.m.	Hostile artillery active during afternoon as was in forward areas. Command of "D" Brigade passes from Major W.R. Rushton, R.F.A. 181st Bge R.F.A. to O.C. 50th Bge R.F.A. Relief of remaining section of batteries completed.	
		6.0 p.m.	Brigade moves from Wayne Farm via LA PANNE to GHYVELDE.	
	30th		Enemy artillery made trouble by aircraft following Casualties — 2 O.Rs killed + 14 O.Rs wounded to 11 horses wounded.	
	31st		Brigade in rest at GHYVELDE.	
	"	"	"	"
	"	"	"	"

Lieut Colonel R.F.A.
Commanding 181st Brigade R.F.A.

WO 95/2625/3
41 DIV
187 BDE RFA
March 1918 - Oct 1919

41st Div.

Bde. returned with
Div. from Italy
8/13.3.18.

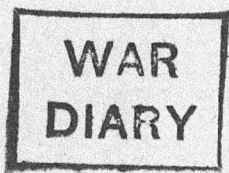

Headquarters,

187th BRIGADE, R.F.A.

M A R C H

1 9 1 8

Army Form C. 2118.

H/Bm
VOL 23

INTELLIGENCE SUMMARY.
(Erase heading not required.)

Instructions regarding War Diaries and Intelligence Summaries are contained in F. S. Regs., Part II. and the Staff Manual respectively. Title pages will be prepared in manuscript.

Place	Date	Hour	Summary of Events and Information	Remarks and references to Appendices
ITALY	March 1st to 3rd		"A", "B" & "D" Batteries in action on MONTELLO under tactical control of 5th I.D.A. on any of routes to the onnect and as March 5th	
	March 4th		"C" Battery with 32nd Brigade R.F.A. (Yth Divisional Artillery) as from 6-2-18. 189th Bgde.R.F.A. & Battery Major Ruis concentrated in RAMON area.	
	Night 4/5th		The aforesaid Batteries cancelled owing to inclement weather, coming over PIAVE then in flood — 189th Bgde.R.F.A. Batteries unchanged from action.	
	5th		Brigade marched from RAMON area to VIA DI VILLA nr TREVISO. Lieut. Colonel E.R.G. Symons D.S.O. R.F.A. assumed command Brigade vice Lieut. Colonel Guy Symonds D.S.O., R.F.A. "Detained in England".	
	6th & 7th		Brigade concentrated in VIA DI VILLA area.	
	8th & 9th		Brigade entrained at TREVISO en route for FRANCE.	
FRANCE	12th & 13th		Detrained at DOULLENS (FRANCE) & concentrated at BEZAINCOURT S. of DOULLENS.	
	14th to 20th		41st & 10th Divisions in G.H.Q. Reserve, & under orders to move within 12 hours notice.	
	21st		German Offensive commenced on ST. QUENTIN – BAPAUME Fronts.	
			Brigade marched from BEZAINCOURT to BEAUCOURT, arriving about 3.0 pm	
	22nd	12.5 pm	Received orders to march to ABLAINZEVILLE area.	
		5.15 pm	Brigade left BEAUCOURT & arrived at ABLAINZEVILLE at 1.30 pm.	
		2.5 pm	Received orders to move into action.	
		3.0 pm	Left ABLAINZEVILLE & moved into action near FAVREUIL under command	

INTELLIGENCE SUMMARY.

(Erase heading not required.)

Instructions regarding War Diaries and Intelligence Summaries are contained in F. S. Regs., Part II. and the Staff Manual respectively. Title pages will be prepared in manuscript.

Place	Date	Hour	Summary of Events and Information	Remarks and references to Appendices
FRANCE	22nd	—	Command of 6th Divisional Artillery, covering 41st & 10th Divisions Infantry, ordered retired RCA 10th Divisional Infantry.	
	23rd	—	Three obstinate attacks by enemy repulsed by Infantry & Artillery barrage.	
	24th	—	Situation on right flank of 10th Divisional front obscure owing to premature ? of enemy at this ??.	
		5:30pm	Orders received for Brigade to retire. (Now under command of 41st Divl Arty)	
Night 24/25th			Brigade retired to position near BIHUCOURT.	
	25th		Further retirement ordered to BUCQUOY. 41st Divl Inf relieved by 62nd Divl Inf.	
	26th	2:0am	Brigade retired & took up position rear of ESSARTS.	
	27th–31st		Brigade covering 62nd Divl Infantry, holding line running through BUCQUOY.	

Casualties during month :— 2 Officers + 3 OR's Killed.
                             2   "   + 38 "   Wounded.

E. W. Cole
Lieut Colonel R.F.A.
Capt.
Commanding 187th Bde R.F.A.

41st Divisional Artillery

187th BRIGADE R.F.A.

APRIL 1 9 1 8

184th Brigade R.F.A.

WAR DIARY
or
INTELLIGENCE SUMMARY

Army Form C. 2118.

April 1918.   WD 23

Place	Date	Hour	Summary of Events and Information	Remarks and references to Appendices
France	April 1st		Brigade in action near ESSARTS (Sheet 57D) as from March 26th, covering 62nd Divisional Infantry, firing line running through BUCQUOY.	
	1st to 4th		No infantry action took place — enemy maintaining position. Hostile artillery activity during this period chiefly confined to roads in back areas. Harassing fire carried out by 18 Batteries nightly.	
	5th	5:30 am	Enemy attacked & succeeded in establishing himself in ROSSIGNOL WOOD. Artillery preparation consisted of some gas shelling of areas near Battery Positions, and 6pdr fire. S.O.S. Barrage from 5:30 am to 11:15 am with great intensity. Bombardier, but owing to exhaustion and of personnel was obliged to remove registration to "B" Battery Sustained 58 casualties including 4 Officers. "B" Battery temporarily out of action from midday until 7-9.0 pm when it was reinforced by "J" R.H.A.G. personnel.	
			37th Divisional Infantry relieved 62nd Divisional Infantry.	
	6th			
	6th to 11th		Front generally quiet. Hostile Artillery active on track towards SUCHEZ – FONQUEVILLERS. Harassing fire carried out nightly on PUISIEUX & vicinity.	

Army Form C. 2118.

WAR DIARY
or
INTELLIGENCE SUMMARY.
(Erase heading not required.)

Instructions regarding War Diaries and Intelligence Summaries are contained in F. S. Regs., Part II. and the Staff Manual respectively. Title pages will be prepared in manuscript.

Place	Date	Hour	Summary of Events and Information	Remarks and references to Appendices
April	18th		62nd Divisional Infantry relieved 37th Divisional Infantry.	
	19th to 22nd		Front generally quiet. Nothing of importance to report.	
	23rd		189th Brigade R.F.A. withdrawn from action into Corps Reserve and concentrated in PAS.	
	24th to 29th		In Corps Reserve.	
	30th		189th Brigade R.F.A. relieves 190th Brigade R.F.A. (HLR D.A.) & takes over command of Rgt Group of 42nd Divisional Artillery, covering 42nd Divisional Infantry.	

E. N. Carl
Lieut Colonel R.F.A.
Commanding 189th Bde R.F.A.

189th Bgde R.F.A.

May 1918

WAR DIARY or INTELLIGENCE SUMMARY
Army Form C. 2118.

(Erase heading not required.)

Place	Date	Hour	Summary of Events and Information	Remarks and references to Appendices
France	1st		189th Brigade R.F.A. covering HPS Divisional Infantry & under tactical command of 2 C.R.A., & 2nd 10 Divisions too from 30-4-18.	
	1st - 5th		Front generally quiet; harassing fire carried out by Batteries nightly on PUISIEUX & vicinity.	
	Night 5/6th		Harris guns in battery withdrawn to Wagon Lines; remaining two from Battery relieved one section per Battery of 235th Brigade F.A., New Zealand Divisions Artillery	
	6/7th		Relief as above completed. 189th Brigade F.A. covering Regt Brigade of New Zealand Division Artillery HEBUTERNE sector.	
	7th		Hostile artillery fairly active - HEBUTERNE shelled intermittently throughout the day & from 6 pm to 8.30 pm.	
	8th to 11th		Harassing fire during night on tracks K.22.C.H.O., K.22.d.30, TOUVENT FARM. Front generally quiet; harassing fire carried out nightly on tracks K.22.c. and d.	
	Night 11/12th		One Section per Battery relieved by one section per Battery of 266 Brigade R.F.A. (57th Divisional Artillery)	
	Night 12/13th		Relief completed - Batteries concentrated in COUIN area	
	14th		Batteries marched to DOULLENS & entrained en route for POPERINGHE area	
	Night 14/15th			
	15th		Detrained at HIDE BECK (near POPERINGHE) & marched on LA LOVIE.	

Army Form C. 2118.

WAR DIARY
or
INTELLIGENCE SUMMARY.
(Erase heading not required.)

Instructions regarding War Diaries and Intelligence Summaries are contained in F. S. Regs., Part II. and the Staff Manual respectively. Title pages will be prepared in manuscript.

Place	Date	Hour	Summary of Events and Information	Remarks and references to Appendices
	Night 16/17th		One section for Battery returns one section for battery 112nd Brigade R.F.A. (33rd Divisional Artillery)	
	Night 17/18th		Relief completed — 167th Brigade R.F.A. covering 123rd Infantry Brigade being line from I.10.c.5.6. – I.21.6.8.9. (Belgium, Sheet 28. N.W.), duties commenced by C.R.A., HINGNO WOODS	
	18th		Batteries carried out registration throughout the day. Hostile artillery firing active – Cross roads YPRES necessary frontiers attention. Back areas heavily shelled during night. Harassing fire, western Brigade fire carried out by 6 batteries during night.	
	19th		Registration continued by 6 batteries. Hostile artillery much quieter. Harassing fire by 6 Batteries during night.	
	20th 12.30 pm		M.F.Gale — T.2.c.0.6. fired on by 6/19 YPRES intermittently shelled during day. Harassing fire by Batteries during night.	
	21st 9.0 am		Enemy fired on our movement at I.29.c.15.65. Hostile artillery very active between 10.0 am & 3.30 pm vicinity of ST. JULIEN's Junction + SALVATION CORNER being heavily shelled by 5.9's	
	Night 21/22nd		Batteries fired barrage in support of raid carried out by 2nd Battalion W.F.I. (6th Division) on I.27.c. and d. + BLAUWEPOORT FARM — 16 Prisoners captured.	

Army Form C. 2118.

WAR DIARY
or
INTELLIGENCE SUMMARY.
(Erase heading not required.)

Instructions regarding War Diaries and Intelligence Summaries are contained in F. S. Regs., Part II. and the Staff Manual respectively. Title pages will be prepared in manuscript.

Place	Date	Hour	Summary of Events and Information	Remarks and references to Appendices
	22nd	5.45 pm	A/161 fired on Working Party at I.30.a.60.10., dispersing same. Units casualties	
		6.0 pm	Batteries fired on Hostile Dumps at I.22.6.34.93. Harassing fire by Batteries during night. A/161 H.M.G. and C. Company shells with gas	
	23rd		A/161 fired on movement in CANADA STREET Trench. Throughout day Hostile artillery was quiet during day. Harassing fire by Batteries during night.	
	24th		Quiet day. — Harassing fire by batteries during night.	
	25th		A/161 fired on movement at I.30.a.8.2. + dugouts in HOOGE. Harassing fire by Batteries during night. Hostile artillery below normal.	
	26th		A/161 fired on movement at I.18.a.8.6. + I.30.c.45.10. Harassing fire by Batteries during night. Hostile artillery active throughout day. Concentrates amount of gas shelling during night on I.11.d. + vicinity.	
	27th	2.00 am 10.0 am	B/161 fire gas on I.18.b.48.74. — I.18.b.48.70. Quiet day, except for desultory shelling of our front area. Harassing fire by Batteries during night.	
	28th	2.0 pm 6.15 pm	B/161 Gas M.E. Gas — I.18.a.90.10. A/161 fired on Trenches on I.18.a. Harassing fire by Batteries during night.	

WAR DIARY
or
INTELLIGENCE SUMMARY.
(Erase heading not required.)

Army Form C. 2118.

Place	Date	Hour	Summary of Events and Information	Remarks and references to Appendices
	29th	5:30am	A/169 fired + dispersed movement at I.30.a.6.6.	
		9.0pm	B/169 fired no movement at I.24.a central. Hostile artillery quiet. Neut. harassing fire carried on during night.	
	30th	11:15pm	C/169 fired 20 rounds at hostile fire forces in firing line. Raid rival travelled very near the place + I was seen to crash at I.17.d.9.6. Area of H.O.B was shelled with 5.9's during morning, otherwise hostile artillery was inactive. Harassing fire carried on during night.	
	31st	9.0am	Working Party at I.30.a dispersed by A/169.	
		7.30pm	B/169 fired no movement at HEDGE STREET Tunnels. Hostile artillery active at intervals during day no fire at night. Harassing Fire carried on during night.	

2-6-18

[signature]
Capt. for Major R.F.A.
Commanding 169 Bde. R.F.A.

WAR DIARY
or
INTELLIGENCE SUMMARY.

(Erase heading not required.)

Army Form C. 2118.

184th Brigade, R.F.A.   June 1918.

Place	Date	Hour	Summary of Events and Information	Remarks and references to Appendices
France	June 1st		Brigade in action as from 17-5-18 covering 122nd Infantry Brigade in Right Sector of Divisional Front, extending from I.10.a.5.6. to I.21.6.2.9. (sheet 28 N.W. BELGIUM). Hostile artillery quiet in Brigade Zone. Batteries carried on harassing fire on roads, tracks, etc. during the night.	
	Night 1/2nd		Batteries fired barrage in support of raid on RIFLE FARM by 10th K.R.R's (123rd Infantry Brigade) — Raiders found trench free of enemy.	
	2nd		A/184 fired an armament on HEDGE STREET Junction traversed N.F. Gase at I.29.6.5.5.	
		9.30 am	B/184's position attacked with 10.5 c.m. How — quantity of ammunition destroyed & one gun slightly damaged. Batteries carried on normal harassing fire during night. 123rd Infantry Brigade relieved by 148th Infantry Brigade (49th Division).	
	Night 2/3rd			
	3rd		A/184's Battery Position shelled — 4 O.R's killed & 4 O.R's wounded. 12th Infantry Brigade (on loan) relieved by 146th Infantry Brigade. A/184 fired an armament strafing tracks at I.29.d. and I.30.a. except for intermittent shelling of YPRES, hostile artillery quiet. Batteries carried on harassing fire during night.	
	Night 3/4th		123rd Infantry Brigade relieved 146th Right Sector, relieved 146th Infantry Brigade.	
	4th		Quiet day — Hostile artillery activity chiefly against Brigade tracks, roads.	

Army Form C. 2118.

WAR DIARY
or
INTELLIGENCE SUMMARY.
(Erase heading not required.)

Instructions regarding War Diaries and Intelligence Summaries are contained in F. S. Regs., Part II. and the Staff Manual respectively. Title pages will be prepared in manuscript.

Place	Date	Hour	Summary of Events and Information	Remarks and references to Appendices
France	Night 4/5th		One section for Battery relieved by one section from Battery B 245th Bay. La.B.B.A. (49th Divisional Artillery)	
	5th		Much harrying fire carried on during night. Our artillery front actively covering enemy activity in back of their front line against enemy Artillery.	
	Night 5/6		Remaining two sections fire Battery relieved by 2 sections from Battery of 245th Bryde. R.F.A. Battery concentrated in wagon Lines.	
	6th		Brigade moved from Wagon Lines to DROGLANDT area (Map – Hazebrouck 5.2)	
	7th		March continued to POLINCOVE CAPPELL.	
	8th		March continued to POLINCOVE area (Second Army Training Area). In Army Reserve	
	9th		Received orders to proceed by road within 2 hours notice	
	10th to 15th		Brigade Foot– Battery Classes in Lines Drill Wiring Drill Signalling	
	16th		Field Day in conjunction with 38th Australian Divisions carried out at LA RONVILLE	
	17th to 24th		Intra – Battery Training Brigade Classes carried out	

Army Form C. 2118.

WAR DIARY
or
INTELLIGENCE SUMMARY.
(Erase heading not required.)

Instructions regarding War Diaries and Intelligence Summaries are contained in F.S. Regs., Part II. and the Staff Manual respectively. Title pages will be prepared in manuscript.

Place	Date	Hour	Summary of Events and Information	Remarks and references to Appendices
France	25th	—	Hd. Divisional Artillery inspected by Second Army Commander — General Sir H. Plumer.	
	26th	—	Brigade arrived from POLINCOVE to ZEGGERS CAPPELL Area.	
	27th	—	Marched onward to ABEELE area.	
	28th	—	Brigade concentrated in ABEELE area.	
	—	—	Brigade moved into Reserve Positions as under:—	
			3rd at L. 27. b. 70. 50.	
			A/104 " L. 28. c. 20. 70.	
			B/104 " L. 28. b. 00. 50. } Sheet 27 (Belgium & France)	
			C/104 " L. 28. d. 50. 60.	
			D/104 " L. 27. b. 30. 50.	
	Night 29th/30th		Gun sections for battery went into action at points mentioned below in relief of 7th Brigade 10 Mounted Artillery.	
			A/104. — M.10.a. 05.15.	
			B/104. — M.9.c. 69.55. } Sheet 27 (Belgium & France)	
			C/104. — M.9.a. 80.95	
			D/104. — N.9.c. 20.65.	
	Night 30th		Second sections for battery went into action at above positions.	

30-6-18

J. Murgul
Lt. Col. Comdt. R.F.A.
Commanding 104th Bde R.F.A.

Army Form C. 2118.

151/M. Brigade R.F.A.   July 1918

WAR DIARY
or
INTELLIGENCE SUMMARY.
(Erase heading not required.)

Place	Date	Hour	Summary of Events and Information	Remarks and references to Appendices
France	1st		Gun sectors for batteries in action of undermentioned points, as from 30-6-18	
			A/151. - M.10.a. 05.15.	
			B/151. - M.9.c. 69.55. } Sheet 24 (Belgium & France)	
			C/151. - N.9.a. 80.95.	
			D/151. - M.9.b. 20.85.	
	Night 1st/2nd		Renewing sectors for batteries went into action at following points :-	
			A/151. - M.10.d. 30.40	
			B/151. - M.10.c. 70.55	
			C/151. - N.10.d. 00.60	
			D/151. - M.10.t. 15.70.	
	2nd	3.0 am	Lieut Colonel C.R.O.G. Bryan D.S.O., R.F.A. assumed command of Brigade, covering 124th Infantry Brigade, being Right Sector of Dismount Front (M.24.d. 10.50 - N.9.a. 35.70). Dismount Front, extending from M.24.d. 10.50 to N.9.c. 35.15. sub-divided into two sub-sectors each by 123, 123 + 124 th Infantry Brigades	
	3rd to 5th		Batteries carried on registration, harassing fire on roads & tracks	
	Night 5/6		Battle artillery activity during the period except [illegible] to frame move forward sectors of A/151 moved from M.10.d. 30.40 to M.10.b. 70.70.	
	6th to 8th		Batteries fired harassing fire. Battle Artillery showed increased activity on north & front. SCHERPENBERG came in for considerable attention.	

Army Form C. 2118.

WAR DIARY
or
INTELLIGENCE SUMMARY.
(Erase heading not required.)

Instructions regarding War Diaries and Intelligence Summaries are contained in F.S. Regs., Part II. and the Staff Manual respectively. Title pages will be prepared in manuscript.

Place	Date	Hour	Summary of Events and Information	Remarks and references to Appendices
France	Night 8/9th		Four gun pieces of A/119 moved from M.10.a. 95.15. to M.3.d. 10.90.	
	9th to 13th		Batteries fired harassing fire on roads & tracks. Enemy artillery very active in the vicinity of C. roads. Battery with RENINGHELST, WESTOUTRE & ground and received considerable attention.	
	14th	6.0am	Batteries fired barrage in co-operation with minor operations by 6th & 33rd Divisions as on 6th. Harassing fire carried on during night.	
	15th & 16th		Batteries fired usual harassing fire on roads & tracks. Battery artillery active during the period. Enemy's batteries on fronts quiet.	
	19th	1.30am	Battery fired barrage in co-operation with raid by 11th Queens on M.13.d.96.10. – N.20.c.27.90. and from N.14.c.7/2.15. – N.14.c.43.64. Harassing fire carried on during night.	
			Hour artillery active with trench mortars on road & tracks in battery area.	
	20th	3.30pm	A/119 fired in active Trench Mortars at N.25.b.20.53, N.25.b.20.95 & N.25.d.10.75. Hostile artillery active throughout the day particularly on B.29.a, and b, which received about 200 rounds from 15 cm hows. Harassing fire on roads & tracks carried out by Batteries during the night.	
	21st	10.55pm	Battery fired concentrated shoots in conjunction with H.A. on hostile trench mortars & mgs.	
	21st	1.50am	Gunch. Preparation fired by Battery at 12.30am, 12.51am, 2.45am & 3.6am. Enemy put down fire during these concentrations.	

(A804) D. B. & L., London, E.C. Wt. W1271/M1731 750,000 5/17 Sch. 52 Forms/C2118/14

Army Form C. 2118.

WAR DIARY
or
INTELLIGENCE SUMMARY.
(Erase heading not required.)

Instructions regarding War Diaries and Intelligence Summaries are contained in F. S. Regs., Part II. and the Staff Manual respectively. Title pages will be prepared in manuscript.

Place	Date	Hour	Summary of Events and Information	Remarks and references to Appendices
France	Sept 22/16		Battery in conjunction with H.A. fired Grouts Patrouches from 15.30 to 15.35 p.m. 12.30 to 12.55 a.m. 12.55 to 12.58 a.m. 2.31 to 2.35 a.m.	
	23rd		Enemy aircraft repeatedly over our lines. Scattered fire during the day with machine & anti-aircraft gun fire into enemy trenches & aeroplanes from our position.	
	24th	1.30am	Battery fired barrage in co-operation with raid by 12th Infantry Brigade, Riffe Rookery Sap from N.14.c.90.70 & N.14.c.85.35.	
			Japan artillery guns active to day, many active on craft as forward area intermittently between 1.30 am and 3.30 am.	
	25th		Battery fired 160 rounds shrapnel on road & enemy during the night. Great activity noted on enemy's craft. Battery again 5.9's between 7.30 am & 9.30 am — on of our aeroplanes in vicinity to descend.	
	Sept 26/16		Blay's trench stations from N.19.c.90.55 to M.13.6.40.20. Battery fires burst barrage fire to enemy counter. Fields artillery intermittently active on WESTHOFE trench & Crate Bailey	
			Guns day Battery in conjunction with H.O. fired 3 min concentration at 12.15 am 12.30 Am 12.53 am & 1.12 am on N.22.c.75.70, N.21.d.7.3, N.21.d.2.4 & N.21.d 3.3	
	27th		Quiet day Battery did some harassing fire at night on enemy wire trenches etc.	

Army Form C. 2118.

WAR DIARY
or
INTELLIGENCE SUMMARY.
(Erase heading not required.)

Instructions regarding War Diaries and Intelligence
Summaries are contained in F. S. Regs., Part II.
and the Staff Manual respectively. Title pages
will be prepared in manuscript.

Place	Date	Hour	Summary of Events and Information	Remarks and references to Appendices
France	28th	12.30pm	Battery fired 5 rounds in co-operation with raid by 26th Battn. on Repr. Seconion on enemy line at M.19.a.80.16. Enemy put down barrage in no mans land immediately on bursts of our Barrage lasts nearly an hour. Battery carried on hostile fire during the night	
	29th	11.30pm	Enemy. The carried on Barrage. During the fires a retaliation occurred. It lasts nearly top. pms. Unfortunately in spite of heavy intensity of fire on our heavy expense to turning fire.	

31/7-16.

[signature] Lieut. Colonel R.F.A.
Commanding 101 Brigade R.F.A.

184th Brigade, R.F.A.

WAR DIARY or INTELLIGENCE SUMMARY

Army Form C. 2118.

August 1918

JM 28

Place	Date	Hour	Summary of Events and Information	Remarks and references to Appendices
France	1st		184th Brigade R.F.A. in action as from 2-7-18 covering 184th Infantry Brigade, Relieving Right Sector of SCHERPENBERG Front, extending from M.24.d.10.50 – N.19.a.30.70. Sheet 28 (Belgium). Batteries carried out concentration shoots during the day. Harassing fire on roads, tracks etc during the night.	
	2nd to 4th		Hostile Artillery displayed good activity in SCHERPENBERG & vicinity throughout the day & action on road tracks in forward area during the night. Batteries carried out registration of newer harassing fires at night. Hostile artillery generally quiet – desultory shelling of back area stations for an hour or so at night.	
	4th	11 pm	Batteries fired barrage in support of raid by 35th Division, an own right, on M.29.b.y.3.	
	5th	8 pm	Batteries supplied covering fire for harassment by Divisional Trench Mortars on N.19.a.45.00	
	6th to 8th		Harassing fire on roads tracks carried on during night. Hostile Artillery quite inactive during the day & night. Registration Harassing fire on roads etc carried on. Hostile Artillery intermittently active on forward area during day & erratic harassing fire at night.	
	8th	12 midnight	Batteries fired barrage in support of straightening front line on Left of Division's Front. Barrage also fired in support of raid in same time by 10 Bn Queens on trenches. M.24.d.35.35. & M.24.d.50.40.	
	9th	11 pt	Brigade gun as Brigade front. Barrack harassing fire being carried out as previous nights.	

Army Form C. 2118.

WAR DIARY
or
INTELLIGENCE SUMMARY.
(Erase heading not required.)

Instructions regarding War Diaries and Intelligence Summaries are contained in F.S. Regs., Part II. and the Staff Manual respectively. Title pages will be prepared in manuscript.

Place	Date	Hour	Summary of Events and Information	Remarks and references to Appendices
France	12th	3.15 am	In cooperation with Heavy Artillery the 7th Divisional Artillery carried out a preparation fire of heavy trench positions, widening of enemy wire, attempting to neutralise grounds East of 1 Divisional Front. Hostile shelling active, no retaliation from strongpoint between 4 am & 5 am. Batteries carried on harassing fire during the night.	
	13th	2.0 am	Counter Preparation returned by batteries.	
			An enemy SCHERPEN BERG attack intervened by battle artillery throughout the day.	
			Harassing fire carried out during the night.	
	14th	3.15 am	Counter Preparation fired by Batteries as an enemy 8/12th Div. was in our lines was found sown by enemy on our front line.	
		8.45 am	Enemy exposed all over front on N.S.b with 6" guns. This entrenched until	
		5.0 pm	during the same attack a large Train N.b.b. ammunition dump was exploded. During the day there was signs of unusual activity of hostile artillery over the Divisional Front.	
			Batteries fired harassing fire on roads & tracks during the night.	
	15th	6.50 pm	Batteries fired a few SOS calls from the air trained at harassing fire during the night.	
			Hostile Artillery very quiet all day.	
	16th	4.15 am	Enemy put down a heavy barrage on our Left Brigade Front & Batteries fired SOS onto H.21 and other enemy fires died down.	
			Hostile Artillery quiet for remainder of the day. Batteries fired harassing fire on roads & tracks during the night.	

WAR DIARY
OF
INTELLIGENCE SUMMARY.
(Erase heading not required.)

Army Form C. 2118.

Place	Date	Hour	Summary of Events and Information	Remarks and references to Appendices
Fanne	11th	10.50 p	Enemy put down a heavy barrage on left (centre Brigade) Batteries fired an SOS barrage. 45 wounded. Counter fire carried on by Batteries. Personnel in section of each Battery 330 Bde R.F.A. (66th D.A.) relieved personnel of on section for battery 184 Brigade R.F.A.	
	15th	6.0 pm	Personnel of remaining two Sections of 330 Bde.F.A. relieved personnel of two sections of 184th Brigade R.F.A. Command passed to O.C. 330th Bde at R.F.A.	
	19th		Two guns in position for Battery for defence of 2nd Position. 184th Brigade R.F.A. & 330th Brigade R.F.D. exchanged Wagon Lines. 184 KTB wg ne Wagon Lines arranged at K. 27. a., c. & d.	
	20th to 24th		Brigade less 1 section for Battery concentrate in Wagon Lines.	
	25th		6 sec occurred to where 330 Brigade R.F.A. in depth 26/26 & 26/27 th	
	Night 25/26th		One section per Battery returned on section per Battery 330 Brigade R.F.A. completed.	
	Night 27/28th		Relief of 330 Bryd R.F.A. completed.	
	29th	3.5 pm	Lieut Col. C.D.G. Pyne. D.S.O. Resumed command of Brigade.	
	28th		Guns in front strengthened army. Harassing fire carried out by Batteries during the night.	

WAR DIARY
or
INTELLIGENCE SUMMARY.

(Erase heading not required.)

Army Form C. 2118.

Instructions regarding War Diaries and Intelligence Summaries are contained in F. S. Regs., Part II. and the Staff Manual respectively. Title pages will be prepared in manuscript.

Place	Date	Hour	Summary of Events and Information	Remarks and references to Appendices
France	29th		There was Harrd during the day & several enemy Krin ponts to a furious cannonade. Enemy fire continued up & Down during the night.	
	30th		Enemy artist fire on nests BAILLEUL, KEMMEL HILL &c. There were frequent hostile enemy aim. Enemy aircraft very active this day.	
	31st		During entire day enemy artillery active on front of Corps on front of Nr. KEMMEL O our troops. — DONEGAL FARM — LINDENHOEK — VIERSTRAAT — VOORMEZEELE. 26 hostile aircraft. Bombs were dropped & fires started on SCHERPENBERG, ZWARTELEEN, KEMMEL, YPRES, ARMENTIERES, MESSINES, TALBENTEN.	

A. W. Long
Lt Col. R.F.A.
Comm'g 107 Bde R.F.A.

WAR DIARY or INTELLIGENCE SUMMARY

Army Form C. 2118.

189th Brigade R.F.A.

September 1918.

Place	Date	Hour	Summary of Events and Information	Remarks and references to Appendices
France	1st		Batteries in action near KEMMEL, having moved forward on 30-8-18, in consequence of enemy withdrawal from KEMMEL HILL.	
	2nd	2pm	Infantry advanced to line N.30.a.5.6. - N.36.a.6.0.	
		3.30 to 4.30pm	Batteries fired barrage.	
	3rd		Infantry advanced to line N.30.a.6.6. & N.30.c.9.1. meeting enemy finally. "B" Battery moved to N.32.a.0.8, but were fired thereon owing to enemy shelling. Patrols sent forward to reach line of Batteries N.24.c. & N.30.a.	
	4th	5.30am	Under covering fire by 189 Brigade R.F.A. & 10th Battery 190 Bde R.F.A, units of 102nd Infantry Brigade (34th Division) attacked to 7.30 am zone line 0.20.a.3.8. along road to 0.20.c.3.2. "A" to 0 reached to line 0.20.a.3.8. along road to T.3.c.5.3 & N.32.c.7.1. Batteries were forward & occupied positions respectively.	
	5th		A/189, B/189 exchanged positions with "A" & "D" Batteries (34th Division) at N.3.c.1.4 & G.22.a.1.4. respectively.	
	6th		B/189 exchanged position with B/160 at N.3.a.4.2.	
	7th		C/189 exchanged position with C/160 at H.32.c.9.0. Brigade covering 123rd Infantry Brigade in DICKEBUSCH SECTOR.	

Army Form C. 2118.

WAR DIARY
or
INTELLIGENCE SUMMARY.

(Erase heading not required.)

Instructions regarding War Diaries and Intelligence Summaries are contained in F. S. Regs., Part II. and the Staff Manual respectively. Title pages will be prepared in manuscript.

Place	Date	Hour	Summary of Events and Information	Remarks and references to Appendices
France	8th		B/109 & A/109 move to position at N.S.C. 5.0. + N.8.a.6.9. respectively. Harassing fire carried on during the night.	
	9th		Generally quiet on front.	
	10th & 11th		Quieter. Several Front Systems Artillery fire attempts to destroy shelling at night on roads and tracks. Harassing fire by 6 attacks during night.	
	18th		132nd Infantry Brigade relieved R3rd Infantry Brig de.	
	19th		Quiet day	
	Nights 19/20 &		6 no sections for battery returned by one section per battery 152nd Army d RFA	
	Night 20/21		" " "	
	Night 21/22		" " "	
			Remaining sections returned by Battery of 152nd Bryade F.A. (34th D.A.)	
			Battere concentrated in Wagon Lines	
	22nd	10 a.m.	Command & Front groups & O.C. 152nd Brigade FA	
			Brigade FOs transferred to BELGIAN CHATEAU (35th Divisional area)	
	Nights 23/24th		3 guns per battery occupied following positions (sibrs)	
			A/109 - H.24.c.77.)	
			B/109 - I.19.c.75.75.) Sheet 28 NW (Belgium)	
			C/109 - H.29.c.9.2.)	
			D/109 - I.14.c.15.80.)	

Army Form C. 2118.

WAR DIARY
or
INTELLIGENCE SUMMARY.
(Erase heading not required.)

Instructions regarding War Diaries and Intelligence Summaries are contained in F. S. Regs., Part II. and the Staff Manual respectively. Title pages will be prepared in manuscript.

Place	Date	Hour	Summary of Events and Information	Remarks and references to Appendices
France	Mar 27/71		Remaining three guns of Battery moved into their position. Lieut Colonel E.B.S. Boyne O/S.O commanding Rgt. Group of 35th Division Arty under orders of C.R.A. 35th Division.	
	28th	5.25 am	Seenh Army in conjunction with Belgian Army on left attacked enemy's frontiers at 9 am & by 10 am had reached a general line PASCHENDAEL – KORTEWILDE (inclusive) Batteries fired barrage, supporting 105th Infantry Brigade (35th Division).	
		Noon to 1 pm	Battery advanced & took up position in RAVINE WOOD.	
	29th	9 am	Batteries ordered to advance & occupy position S.E. of HOLLEBEKE CHATEAU to support attack in direction of COMINES.	
		5 pm	Fired S.O.S. — Enemy counter attack. Thereupon fire maintained throughout the night.	
	30th	5.35 am	Batteries fired barrage in support of attack by 41st Division on COMINES. Infantry reported in COMINES at 7h 5 am.	

M?urel Capt.
for Lieut Colonel R.F.A.
Commanding 161 Brigade R.F.A.

190th Brigade R.F.A.   October 1918.   Army Form C. 2118.

WAR DIARY
or
INTELLIGENCE SUMMARY.
(Erase heading not required.)

Place	Date	Hour	Summary of Events and Information	Remarks and references to Appendices
France	1st		Batteries in action in area S.E. of HOLLEBEKE CHATEAU as from 27-9-18. Batteries moved to AMERIKA (28/P.12.d.) to support attack on GHELUWE SWITCH.	
		6.15pm	Attack made on GHELUWE SWITCH — unsuccessful.	
	2nd	3.30pm	Batteries fired barrage in support of attack on GHELUWE SWITCH.	
		6.15pm	Enemy counter attack — SOS fired during which time Batteries were subjected to intense fire from 8" Howitzers. "A" & "C" Batteries lost 3 guns + one gun respectively knocked out.	
			Harassing fire carried on by Batteries during the night.	
	3rd		One section per battery retained one section per battery. 17 Brigade R.F.A. in 28/J.30.	
	4th		Relief of 17 Royal R.F.A. completed. Brigade covering 14th Division Infantry being in action GHELUWE Front.	
	5th to 12th		Days unchanged. Enemy artillery increased in activity, & battery areas were frequently subjected to sharp bursts of fire from all calibres.	
	13th		Batteries moved to Battle Positions in K.33.a.+c.	
	14th	5.35am	Second Army in co-operation with Belgian Army on left attacked. Batteries fired barrage supporting 41st Division Infantry.	
		9.30am	Batteries advanced to forward positions at L.31.a. + L.N. of MENIN.	
	15th		Batteries withdrawn to Wagon Lines in K.23.a. +c.	

Army Form C. 2118.

WAR DIARY
or
INTELLIGENCE SUMMARY.
(Erase heading not required.)

Place	Date	Hour	Summary of Events and Information	Remarks and references to Appendices
France	16th	9 am	Battery marched from Major Lewis & rejoined 173rd Brigade R.F.A. (36th Division) coming COURTRAI from in J.15 N.d. GULLEGHEM.	
	17th		Front unchanged. "B", "C" & "D" Batteries moved to J.16.	
	18th 19th		Patrols pushed out into COURTRAI which was found to be free from enemy. B batteries in action during this period.	
	20th		Brigade moved from J.15 to N.14. S.E. of MARCKE. (Belgium 27 S.W.)	
	21st	6 am	Brigade moved into action in N.29 & fired in support of attack on ST. GENOIS	
		4 pm	Brigade moved forward to U.9.a. (27 S.W.)	
	22nd	9 pm	Batteries fired in support of attack on MOEN & HEESTERT.	
	23rd	11 am	Brigade relieved by 96th A.F.A. Brigade (att 34th Division)	
		9 pm	Brigade relieved 19th Brigade R.F.A. (29th Division) in O.4.c. (27 S.W.)	
	24th	2.15 am	Fired barrage in support of attack on BOSSUYT. Barrel in 0.29.c – 0.30.c.	
	25th	9 am	Fired barrage in support of attack on Rine L'ESCAUT	
	26th 27th	to 29th	Brigade withdrew from action & marched to new area in M.14. & M.12. (27 S.W.) Brigade concentrated in M.14. & M.12.	

Army Form C. 2118.

WAR DIARY
or
INTELLIGENCE SUMMARY.
(Erase heading not required.)

Instructions regarding War Diaries and Intelligence Summaries are contained in F.S. Regs., Part II. and the Staff Manual respectively. Title pages will be prepared in manuscript.

Place	Date	Hour	Summary of Events and Information	Remarks and references to Appendices
France	29th	2pm	One gun from battery went into action in P. 33.a.10.	
	30th		Remaining guns went into action at same point.	
	31st	6.30	Battery fired Smoke Barrage in support of attack by 35th Division on WOESTEN — KERKHOVE — HAELENDRIES.	

31-10-18

Maud Col. RA
A/Lieut Col. RFA
Commanding 187 A.W.87A

81st Bde R.F.A.

November 1918 Army Form C. 2118.

WAR DIARY
or
INTELLIGENCE SUMMARY.
(Erase heading not required.)

Instructions regarding War Diaries and Intelligence Summaries are contained in F.S. Regs., Part II. and the Staff Manual respectively. Title pages will be prepared in manuscript.

Place	Date	Hour	Summary of Events and Information	Remarks and references to Appendices
France	1st		Battery in action position 30/13-18 in P.33.a.10. (Sheet 29 Bert Furry)	
	2nd		Brigade side-slipped left & relieved 157 Brigade R.F.A. (35th Division) in P.6. 41st Divisional Infantry took over 35th Division Front.	
	3rd to 5th (inc)		Front generally quiet. Batteries carried out harassing fire & wire-cutting, stores (Artillery during this period, maintained an active attitude) not a rifle tiny clock Brigade	
	6th to 9th (inc)		Infantry patrols report retirement of enemy from bank of the SCHELDT.	
	9th		Brigade under orders to move forward in support of 124th Infantry Brigade.	
	10th		Brigade crossed with 123rd Infantry Brigade across SCHELDT to area of M.23. (Sheet 30)	
	11th		Brigade moved with 124th Infantry Brigade having work intention of the latter to force through 123rd Infantry Brigade & came into action E. of NEDERBRAKEL 30/N.14.b. Information received that Armistice had been signed & hostilities ceased as from 11 am. Brigade concentrated in NEDERBRAKEL	
	12th		Brigade marched to GEMELDORP "B" "D" Batteries in action covering bridge over DENDRE. "A" "C" Batteries via Notre Dame JG. at SCHENDELBEKE. (Sheet 30)	
	13th to 14th		Brigade concentrated at GEMELDORP.	

Army Form C. 2118.

WAR DIARY
or
INTELLIGENCE SUMMARY.
(Erase heading not required.)

Instructions regarding War Diaries and Intelligence Summaries are contained in F. S. Regs., Part II. and the Staff Manual respectively. Title pages will be prepared in manuscript.

Place	Date	Hour	Summary of Events and Information	Remarks and references to Appendices
November	18th		Brigade marched, incl. 124th Infantry Brigade Group to NIEUWENHOVE. HQrs at DINDERWINDEKE (Sheet 30)	
	19th		Concentrated in area as above.	
	20th		Marched with Infantry Brigade – Batteries concentrated at VIANE (Sheet 30, V.29.) HQrs at BURGH (Sheet 25, D.12.c)	
	21st to 30th	30th	} Brigade concentrated as above.	

M. Hall Capt
Lieut Colonel R.F.A
Commanding 161st Brigade R.F.A.

161 Brigade R.F.A.

Army Form C. 2118.

WAR DIARY
INTELLIGENCE SUMMARY.
(Erase heading not required.)

December 1918.

Place	Date	Hour	Summary of Events and Information	Remarks and references to Appendices
BELGIUM	1st to 12th		Brigade concentrated in VIRNE area. (About 30 Belgiums as from 20th November 1918)	
	13th		Brigade marched to CLABECQ (Sheet - Brussels).	
	14th		Brigade marched to OPHAIN.	
	15th to 16th		Concentrated in OPHAIN area.	
	17th		Brigade marched to SART DAME AVELINES.	
	18th		Brigade marched to ST. MARTEN.	
	19th		Brigade marched to NOVILLE LES BOIS.	
	20th		Brigade marched to MARNEFFE (Sheet - LIEGE).	
	21st to 31st		Concentrated in MARNEFFE area	

W.E. Fullerton
for Major R.F.A.
Commanding 161 Bde R.F.A.

187th. Brigade, R.F.A.

Army Form C. 2118.

JANUARY, 1919.

WAR DIARY
or
INTELLIGENCE SUMMARY.
(Erase heading not required.)

Instructions regarding War Diaries and Intelligence Summaries are contained in F. S. Regs., Part II. and the Staff Manual respectively. Title pages will be prepared in manuscript.

Place	Date	Hour	Summary of Events and Information	Remarks and references to Appendices
BELGIUM	1st. to 12th.		Brigade concentrated in MARNEFFE Area (W. of LIEGE) as from 20-12-18.	
	13th. to 15th.		Brigade entrained at HUY and ANDENNE for GERMANY, (ARMY OF OCCUPATION).	
	14th. to 16th.		Brigade relieved 14th. Brigade Canadian Field Artillery in COLOGNE area. A/187th. Brigade R.F.A. in position at OBERSTEEG (Sheet 2.L, Germany, 1/100,000) covering 124th. Infantry Brigade holding outpost line. Remaining batteries concentrated in KALK area.	
	17th. to 30th.		Concentrated as above.	
	31st.		B/187th. Brigade R.F.A. relieved A/187th. Brigade, R.F.A. in position at OBERSTEEG.	

31-1-19.

Lieut. Colonel, R.F.A.,
Commanding 187th. Brigade, R.F.A.

187th. Brigade, R.F.A.

FEBRUARY, 1919.

Army Form C. 2118.

WAR DIARY
or
INTELLIGENCE SUMMARY.
(Erase heading not required.)

Place	Date	Hour	Summary of Events and Information	Remarks and references to Appendices
GERMANY.	1st.		Three Batteries of Brigade concentrated in COLOGNE area as from 16th. January. B/187 in position, covering Outpost Line of 124th. Infantry Brigade, at OBERSTEEG (Sheet 2.I.) Germany/10000	
	14th.		C/187 relieved B/187 in position at OBERSTEEG.	
	28th.		D/187 relieved C/187 in position at OBERSTEEG.	
	28-2-19.			

[signature]
Capt for Major, R.F.A.
Commanding 187th. Brigade, R.F.A.

181½ Brigade R.F.A

WAR DIARY
or
INTELLIGENCE SUMMARY.
(Erase heading not required.)

March 1919

Army Form C. 2118

Instructions regarding War Diaries and Intelligence Summaries are contained in F. S. Regs., Part II. and the Staff Manual respectively. Title pages will be prepared in manuscript.

Place	Date	Hour	Summary of Events and Information	Remarks and references to Appendices
Germany	1st		Brigade concentrated in Cologne area. D/181 in postns at OBERSTEE G. Outpost Force relieved by 124th Infantry Brigade.	
	14th		A/181 relieved D/181 in postns at OBERSTEE G.	
	26th		B/181 relieved A/181 in postns at OBERSTEE G. 123rd Infantry Brigade relieved 124th Infantry Brigade. 181st Brigade R.F.A. became attached to 123rd Infantry Brigade as from 26-3-19.	
	31-3-19			

Signed,
Lieut Colonel R.F.A.
Commanding 181st Brigade R.F.A.

Q1097

182nd Brigade, R.F.A.

April 1919

Army Form C. 2118.

WAR DIARY
or
INTELLIGENCE SUMMARY.
(Erase heading not required.)

Place	Date	Hour	Summary of Events and Information	Remarks and references to Appendices
Germany	April 1st		Brigade concentrated in Cologne area less "B" Battery.	
			B/182 Brigade R.F.A. in fortress at OBERSTEES covering Cologne Bridgehead. (now designated as 2nd London Infantry Brigade)	
	11th		C/182 returned B/182 at OBERSTEES.	
	25th		D/182 returned C/182 at OBERSTEES	
April	10th		Lt Colonel J.D. Meiklea, R.H.A.(T) assumed command of Brigade vice Lt Colonel B.D.O. Ryan D.S.O., R.F.A. to England.	
30-4-19				

Staunton Meiklea
Lieut Colonel R.F.A.
for Lieut Colonel R.F.A.
Commanding 182 Brigade R.F.A.

181st Brigade R.A.

Army Form C. 2118.

WAR DIARY
or
INTELLIGENCE SUMMARY.

(Erase heading not required.)

May, 1919.

Place	Date	Hour	Summary of Events and Information	Remarks and references to Appendices
Germany	May 1st		Brigade concentrated in Cologne Area, less "D" Battery. B/181st Brigade R.F.A. in position at OBERSTEEG covering without line held by 2nd London Infantry Brigade.	
	7th		A/181 relieved B/181 at OBERSTEEG.	
	30th		Major J. G. Marsden D.S.O. M.C. R. of A. assumed command of B/181 Bty. vice Capt. (A/Maj) Whyte-Meurlees M.C. R.F.A. to England on leave.	

31st May, 1919.

Marsden Maj.
Lt Colonel R.F.A. (T.F.)
Commanding 181st Brigade R.F.A.

187th Brigade, R.F.A.

WAR DIARY or INTELLIGENCE SUMMARY

Army Form C. 2118.

May, 1919

Place	Date	Hour	Summary of Events and Information	Remarks and references to Appendices
Germany	May 1st		Brigade concentrated in Cologne Area, less "D" Battery of 151st Brigade R.F.A. in position at OBERSTEEG, covering outpost line held by 2nd London Infantry Brigade.	
	9th		D/187 relieved D/151 at OBERSTEEG	
	20th		Major J. C. Marsden D.S.O, M.C., R.F.A. assumed command of B/187 vice Capt (A/Maj) W.H.B. Muirlees M.C., R.F.A., to England on leave.	

31st May, 1919.

Maurice Walsh
Lt. Colonel R.F.A. (T)
Commanding 187 Brigade R.F.A.

181st Brigade, R.F.A.   June, 1919

Army Form C. 2118.

WAR DIARY
or
INTELLIGENCE SUMMARY.
(Erase heading not required.)

Place	Date	Hour	Summary of Events and Information	Remarks and references to Appendices
Germany	June 1st		Brigade concentrated in Cologne Area, less "H" Battery A/181, Brigade R.F.A. in position at OBERSTEEG, covering outpost line held by 2nd London Infantry Brigade.	
	" 13		B/181 relieved A/181. The former going to OBERSTEEG the latter to ELK.	
	" 16		C/181 in accordance with orders received for batteries to move to the Iserlohn Concentration Area, moved from OSTHEIM to OVERATH.	
	" 17		Brigade H'drs, A/181 and D/181 Bde R.F.A. joined the 2nd London Brigade Group (the leading Brigade Group) at ENGELSKIRCHEN. Brigade H'drs moved from HOHENBERG to ENGELSKIRCHEN. A/181 moved from ELK to ENGELSKIRCHEN	
	18/181	"	" OVERATH to —do—	
	B/181	"	" OBERSTEEG to SULTZ —do—	
	C/181	"	" PORZ —do—	

[CONTD.

184 Brigade R.F.A. (Sheet 2)

Army Form C. 2118.

WAR DIARY or INTELLIGENCE SUMMARY

June, 1919.

(Erase heading not required.)

Place	Date	Hour	Summary of Events and Information	Remarks and references to Appendices
Germany	June 18th		B/184 & C/184 Bde R.F.A. (under the command of Major A. Wilson B/184 R.F.A.) joined the 2nd London Brigade Group (the 4th Bde Brigade Group) at UNTER VILKERATH.	
"	24		Orders received that in the event of Peace being signed without any further advance taking place, orders may be expected for all Bde to resume Peace Regt. dispositions as located prior to the move this day to be notified later.	
"	28		Peace was signed at VERSAILLES	
"	30		"Y" Day 184 Brigade R.F.A. from forward concentration Area to normal Billeting Area. Hd qrs 184 Bde R.F.A. from ENGELSKIRCHEN to HOHENBERG	
			A/184 Bde R.F.A. from ENGELSKIRCHEN to EIL	
			B/184 " " " " PORZ	
			D/184 " " UNTERVILKERATH to OBERSTEEG	
			C/184 " " " " ? OVERATH	

30th June, 1919.

[signature]
Lt Colonel R.F.A. (T)
Commdg 184 Bde R.F.A.

187th Brigade, R.F.A. June, 1919

WAR DIARY or INTELLIGENCE SUMMARY

Army Form C. 2118.

Place	Date	Hour	Summary of Events and Information	Remarks and references to Appendices
Germany	June 1st		Brigade concentrated in Cologne Area, less "A" Battery A/187 F. Brigade R.F.A. in position at OBERSTEEG, covering outpost like held by 2nd London Infantry Brigade.	
	13		B/187 relieved A/187, the former going to OBERSTEEG the latter to Elk.	
	16		C/187, in accordance with orders received for batteries to move to the Thousand Concentration Area, moved from OSTHEIM to OVERATH	
	17		Brigade Hdqrs., A/187 and B/187 Bde R.F.A. joined the 2nd London Brigade Group (the leading Brigade Group) at ENGELSKIRCHEN. Brigade Hdqrs. moved from HOHENBERG to ENGELSKIRCHEN	
			A/187 moved from Elk to ENGELSKIRCHEN	
	18/187	"	" OVERATH to —do—	
	13/187	"	" OBERSTEEG to SULTZ —do—	
	C/187	"	" PORZ " —do—	

[CONTD.

184 Brigade R.F.A. (Sheet 2)

WAR DIARY
or
INTELLIGENCE SUMMARY.
(Erase heading not required.)

Army Form C. 2118.

June 1919

Place	Date	Hour	Summary of Events and Information	Remarks and references to Appendices
Germany	June 18th	9/18	Instructions received that the advance of Hon'ble General of the 2nd London Brigade Group (the 184 Brigade Group) at UNTER VILKERATH.	
	24		Orders received that on the Treaty of Peace being signed without any further advance being made, and owing to the Schedule for cut back to peace Establishments in readiness prior to the move this day to be notified as "Z" day.	
	28		Peace was signed at VERSAILLES	
	30		"Z" day 184 Brigade R.F.A. from forward consolidation area to forward Billeting area. A/184 Bde R.F.A. from ENGELSKIRCHEN to HOHENBERG	
			B/184 Bde R.F.A. from ENGELSKIRCHEN to EIL	
			C/184 " " " " " PORZ	
			D/184 " " UNTER VILKERATH to OBERSTEEG	
			184 " " -do- to OVERATH	

30th June, 1919.

Hamilton Miller
Lt Colonel R.F.A.
Commdg 184 Bde R.F.A.

187th Brigade R.F.A.

WAR DIARY
or
INTELLIGENCE SUMMARY.
(Erase heading not required.)

Army Form C. 2118.

July 1919

Place	Date	Hour	Summary of Events and Information	Remarks and references to Appendices
Germany	July 1st		Brigade concentrated in Cologne Area Nos "B" and "C" Batteries.	
			B/187 Brigade R.F.A in position at OBERSTEEG	
			C/187 " " at OYERATH	
	2.		C/187 Brigade R.F.A moved from OYERATH to normal Billeting Area at OSTHEIM	
	10.		B/187 Brigade R.F.A moved from position at OBERSTEEG to normal Billeting Area at HOHENBERG.	
	19.		The Brigade fired a Salute of 21 Guns from West Bank of Rhine just N of HOHENZOLLERN BRIDGE, Cologne, in commemoration of the signing of Peace	

31st July 1919.

J S Backwith
Major R.F.A
Commanding 187 Bde R.F.A

187th Brigade R.F.A.

WAR DIARY
or
INTELLIGENCE SUMMARY.
(Erase heading not required.)

Army Form C. 2118.

July 1919

Place	Date	Hour	Summary of Events and Information	Remarks and references to Appendices
Germany	July 1st		Brigade concentrated in Cologne Area less "B" and "C" Batteries.	
			B/187 Brigade, R.F.A. in position at OBERSTEEG C/187 " " at OYERATH	
	2		C/187 Brigade R.F.A. moved from OYERATH to normal Billeting Area at OSTHEIM.	
	10		B/187 Brigade R.F.A. moved from position at OBERSTEEG to normal Billeting Area at HOHENBERG.	
	19		The Brigade fired a salute of 21 Guns from West Bank of Rhine just N of HOHENZOLLERN BRIDGE Cologne in commemoration of the signing of Peace	
	31st July 1919.			J S Barlworth Major R.F.A. Commanding 187th Bde R.F.A.

187th Brigade R.F.A.

WAR DIARY
or
INTELLIGENCE SUMMARY.
(Erase heading not required.)

Army Form C. 2118.

August, 1919.

Place	Date	Hour	Summary of Events and Information	Remarks and references to Appendices
Germany	Aug 1st		Brigade concentrated in Cologne Area.	
	2/18.7		A/187 Brigade R.F.A. at Elb.	
	3/18.7		B/ do - " HOHENBERG	
	4/18.7		C/ do - " OSTHEIM	
	5/18.7		D/ do - " PORZ	

J.O.Brunwarth
Major R.F.A.
Commanding 187th Bde R.F.A.

187th Brigade R.F.A.

Army Form C. 2118.

WAR DIARY
or
INTELLIGENCE SUMMARY.
(Erase heading not required.)

August, 1919

Place	Date	Hour	Summary of Events and Information	Remarks and references to Appendices
Germany	Aug. 1st		187 Brigade concentrated in Cologne Area	
			A/187 Brigade, R.F.A. at Elw. HOHENBERG	
			B/187 — do — " OSTHEIM	
			C/187 — do — " OSTHEIM	
			D/187 — do — " PORZ	

J S Borthwick
Major R.F.A.
Commanding 187th Bde R.F.A.

187th Brigade R.A.

WAR DIARY
or
INTELLIGENCE SUMMARY.
(Erase heading not required.)

Army Form C. 2118.

September 1919

Place	Date	Hour	Summary of Events and Information	Remarks and references to Appendices
Germany	1st		Brigade concentrated in Cologne Area:-	
			A/187 Brigade R.F.A. at EIL	
			B/187 " " " HOHENBURG	
			C/187 " " " OSTHEIM	
			D/187 " " " PORZ	

Hamilton Wickes
Lt. Colonel R.F.A. (T)
Commanding 187th Brigade R.F.A.

/181st Brigade R.F.A

Army Form C. 2118.

WAR DIARY
or
INTELLIGENCE SUMMARY.

September 1919

Place	Date	Hour	Summary of Events and Information	Remarks and references to Appendices
Germany	1st		Brigade concentrated in Cologne Area:-	
			A/181 Brigade R.F.A at Elm	
	2/181		" " " " Hohenburg	
	5/181		" " " " Ostheim	
	6/181		" " " "	
	D/181		" " " " Porz	

Staunton McKh Lt Colonel R.F.A (T)
Commanding 181st Brigade R.F.A

Army Form C. 2118.

WAR DIARY
INTELLIGENCE SUMMARY.
(Erase heading not required.)

187th Brigade, R.F.A.

Instructions regarding War Diaries and Intelligence Summaries are contained in F. S. Regs., Part II. and the Staff Manual respectively. Title pages will be prepared in manuscript.

Place	Date	Hour	Summary of Events and Information	Remarks and references to Appendices
KALK, Near COLOGNE Germany	14-10-19.		Nothing of interest to report during month of OCTOBER 1919 except:- Batteries and Headquarters of 187th Brigade, R.F.A. moved to RHIEL/ ARTILLERY Barracks. NIPPES.	
	25-10-19.		Remaining personnel of 187th and 190th Brigade, R.F.A. along with personnel of Lancashire Divisional Artillery, and London D.A.C., are now consolidated to form the Royal Field Artillery, RHINE GARRISON, all Officers being on Regular Commission service. Old Officers have been dispersed through Concentration Camp.	Appendix 1.

[signature] Capt R.F.A.
for
Colonel.
Commanding Royal Field Artillery,
RHINE GARRISON.

MOVEMENTS OF OFFICERS- OCTOBER 1919.

187th BRIGADE, ROYAL FIELD ARTILLERY.

POSTINGS. - 25-10-19.

Colonel R.G.KEYWORTH, DSO. to command Brigade,
                           from Lancs.D.A.
Major C.A.L.BROWNLOW, DSO. to A/187 from London D.A.
Major J.S.BARKWORTH,   .. B/187   ::   ::
Major C.E.G.WOOLLCOMBE-ADAMS,.. C/187   ::   ::
Lt-Col.A.F.THOMSON, DSO.   .. D/187   ::   ::
Capt.K.P.ATKINSON, MC.   .. A/187   :: Northern D.A.
Capt.H.PRICE WILLIAMS, DSO.MC.:: B/187   :: London D.A.
Capt.A.WITHAM, DSO.   .. C/187   :: Lancs.D.A.
Capt.W.M.MATHESON, DSO.(Adjt):: D/187   :: London D.A.
Capt.H.T.LENNARD,(Adjt)   .. HQ/187   :: Light D.A.
Lieut.S.C.D'AUBUZ,   .. HQ/187   :: London D.A.
Lieut.J.J.MUSKETT,   :: A/187   ::   ::
Lieut.A.F.STANCOMBE,   :: A/187   ::   ::
Lieut.W.H.BORDASS, MC.   :: A/187   ::   ::
2/Lieut.C.A.SPARKES,   :: B/187   ::   ::
Lieut.E.BRANDISH, MC.   :: B/187   ::   ::
Lieut.J.N.PURDON,   :: B/187   :: Northern D.A.
Lieut.E.G.S.CHAMPNEYS,   :: B/187   ::   ::
2/Lieut.D.A.J.BOWIE   :: C/187   ::   ::
Lieut.R.DARLEY, MC.   :: C/187   :: Light D.A.
Lieut.R.V.HUME,   :: C/187   :: London D.A.
2/Lieut.J.H.NEEDHAM,   :: D/187   ::   ::
Lieut.M.DUKE,   :: D/187   ::   ::
Lieut.M.F.T.BAINES,   :: D/187   ::   ::
2/Lieut.C.LAWLOR,   :: D/187   ::   ::

DEMOBILIZATION ETC. - 25-10-19.

Lieut-Col.J.H.MEIKLE, DSO (RHA) T. Relinquished command of Bde.
Lieut.H.MILLS, MC.   )
Lieut.R.H.THOMPSON,   )
2/Lieut.J.DAVIDSON,   )
Lieut.B.PITT,   )
Lieut.J.F.DARE, DCM.   )
Lieut.G.H.THOMPSON,   ) Proceeded to CONCENT for purpose
Lieut.A.H.CLUTTON, MC.   ) of Demobilization 25-10-19.
Lieut.G.E.CLAYTON, MC.   )
Lieut.F.V.WHITE, MC.   )
Lieut.B.G.DARBY, MC.   )
Lieut.K.A.RYDE, MC.   )
Lieut.xxxxxxxxxx,   )

Army Form C. 2118.

WAR DIARY
187th Brigade, R.F.A.
INTELLIGENCE SUMMARY.

(Erase heading not required.)

Instructions regarding War Diaries and Intelligence Summaries are contained in F. S. Regs., Part II. and the Staff Manual respectively. Title pages will be prepared in manuscript.

Place	Date	Hour	Summary of Events and Information	Remarks and references to Appendices
KALK, Near COLOGNE Germany	14-10-19.		Nothing of interest to report during month of OCTOBER 1919 except:-	
			Batteries and Headquarters of 187th Brigade, R.F.A. moved to RHIEL ARTILLERY Barracks. NIPPES	
	25-10-19.		Remaining personnel of 187th and 190th Brigade, R.F.A. along with personnel of Lancashire Divisional Artillery, and London D.A.C., are now consolidated to form the Royal Field Artillery, RHINE GARRISON, all Officers being on Regular Commission service. Old Officers have been dispersed through Concentration Camp.	Appendix 1.

Bernard
Capt. R.F.A.
for
Lt. Colonel.
Commanding Royal Field Artillery,
RHINE GARRISON.

MOVEMENTS OF OFFICERS - OCTOBER 1919.

187th BRIGADE, ROYAL FIELD ARTILLERY.

POSTINGS. - 25-10-19.

Colonel R.G.KEYWORTH, DSO.	to command Brigade, from Lancs.D.A.	
Major C.A.L.BROWNLOW, DSO.	to A/187	from London D.A.
Major J.S.BARKWORTH,	B/187	" " "
Major C.E.G.WOOLLCOMBE-ADAMS,	C/187	" " "
Lt-Col.A.F.THOMSON, DSO.	D/187	" " "
Capt.K.P.ATKINSON, MC.	A/187	" " "
Capt.H.PRICE WILLIAMS, DSO.MC.	B/187	Northern D.A.
Capt.A.WITHAM, DSO.	C/187	London D.A.
Capt.W.M.MATHESON, DSO.MC.	D/187	Lancs.D.A.
Capt.H.T.LENNARD, (Adjt)	HQ/187	London D.A.
Lieut.S.C.D'AUBUZ,	HQ/187	Light D.A.
Lieut.J.J.MUSKETT,	A/187	London D.A.
Lieut.A.F.STANGOMBE,	A/187	" " "
Lieut.W.H.BORDASS, MC.	A/187	" " "
2/Lieut.C.A.SPARKES,	B/187	" " "
Lieut.E.BRANDISH, MC.	B/187	" " "
Lieut.J.N.PURDON,	B/187	Northern D.A.
Lieut.E.G.S.CHAMPNEYS,	B/187	" " "
2/Lieut.D.A.J.BOWIE,	C/187	" " "
Lieut.R.DARLEY, MC.	C/187	Light D.A.
Lieut.R.V.HUME,	C/187	London D.A.
2/Lieut.J.H.NEEDHAM,	D/187	" " "
Lieut.M.DUKE,	D/187	" " "
Lieut.M.F.T.BAINES,	D/187	" " "
2/Lieut.C.LAWLOR.	D/187	" " "

DEMOBILIZATION ETC. - 25-10-19.

Lieut-Col.J.H.MEIKLE, DSO (RHA) T. Relinquished command of Bde.
Lieut.H.MILLS, MC.)
Lieut.R.H.THOMPSON)
2/Lieut.J.DAVIDSON,)
Lieut.B.PITT,)
Lieut.J.F.DARE, DCM.)
Lieut.G.H.THOMPSON,)
Lieut.A.H.CLUTTON, MC.) Proceeded to CONCENT for purpose
Lieut.G.E.CLAYTON, MC.) of Demobilization 25-10-19.
Lieut.F.V.WHITE, MC.)
Lieut.B.G.DARBY, MC.)
Lieut.K.A.RYDE, MC.)

www.ingramcontent.com/pod-product-compliance
Lightning Source LLC
Chambersburg PA
CBHW081539160426
43191CB00011B/1794